KU-715-044

WITHDRAWN FROM STOCK

CONTENTS

Introduction

INTRODUCTION

For many parents of a disabled child, the experience is made all the more traumatic by a lack of information and insensitivity from professionals. Not only do parents feel shocked, saddened and alone by the fact that their child has been diagnosed as having a disability - if a diagnosis at all is made - they are made to feel powerless by a lack of information about their child's condition and the services, support and benefits to which they and their child are entitled.

If you are one of these parents, I hope you will find this book useful and help you to ask for the things which exist to /assist and support you and your child. Because of the wide range of different conditions, this book does not give any information on specific disabilities. This information can be obtained from libraries or organisations such as MENCAP or Contact a Family (see section on useful addresses). Instead this book is a practical guide for parents of children who have any sort of disability, such as a physical disability, a serious chronic health problem or a learning disability (mental handicap), as most of the information presented applies to all families. You will find information here on some of the reactions and emotions most families experience when having a disabled child, welfare benefits, the sorts of services and professionals who are out there to help, the law, holidays, transport, equipment, education and the transition from childhood to adulthood and many of the issues this period brings.

'Caring for a Disabled Child', whilst aimed primarily at parents, may also be of interest to those who work with families of disabled children, whether this is in the health, education or social services. In my experience, many families find the support and advice from a national or voluntary organisation, such as those already mentioned, particularly helpful. This book, therefore, may also be of use to staff working in such agencies. It may also be of use to students of health and social care courses, nursing , nursery nursing and social work.

A word about terms used in this book. There has been much debate about whether it is correct to say 'child with a disability' as this, many argue, emphasises the fact that the child is a child first and foremost and has a disability second. Others argue that children and adults are disabled by society, not because they have an impairment: if society (in the western world anyway) worked in a different way then children and adults with physical or mental impairments would not be disabled. This argument emphasises disability as a social construction and therefore says that it is important to say that these children and adults are 'disabled'. There are important messages in both of these terms so I shall be using them both throughout the book. This book does not set out to discuss the issues of disability in society; instead it is a practical guide, which I think will be of great value to parents and anyone else interested in caring for a disabled child.

Finally and most importantly, many parents of disabled children, both those who have received a specific diagnosis for their child and those who have not, have told me that getting information about and access to services and benefits is a real battle. I hope very much that 'Caring for a Disabled Child' makes some of that battle a little easier for you to fight and eventually win.

1

REACTIONS AND EMOTIONS

When you have a disabled child you have to cope not only with practical issues, such as dealing with benefits and professionals, but also with your emotions and reactions to having a child with a disability and the feelings of relatives and friends. It is also important to consider the reactions and emotions of your disabled child's siblings.

One word of warning before starting to outline the varied reactions and emotions of different people: many of these feelings are negative ones. Although it is natural to feel negative about your child's disability as an initial reaction, remember that it isn't all bad. Children who are disabled - like all children - are both challenging and rewarding. They can bring enormous joy, and witnessing progress in their development, however small, can be wonderful.

REACTIONS AND EMOTIONS OF PARENTS

Some parents are given the news that their child has a disability at birth or even before birth. Others receive a diagnosis after months or years, often suspecting that 'something' was wrong from an early age. Others never receive a diagnosis as their child has no specific condition. Depending on the timing of discovering your child's disability and the way in which you discovered it, your feelings and reactions will vary in nature and intensity. However, most parents go through many of the same emotions that would be felt had they experienced bereavement. These emotions include: immediate grief, shock, disbelief, denial, anger, feeling alone and finally, acceptance and adjustment.

If you were told at your child's birth that s/he had a disability, your shock and grief may have been particularly intense. This is because when most parents are expecting a baby, they are expecting a 'normal' and 'perfect' baby. After 9 months, adjusting to a baby, whether or not s/he is disabled, is a major task. If you have been told that your child will have extra needs, this period of adjustment will be even greater.

The way in which you were told about your child's disability would have had an important effect on your emotions when dealing with the news. Most parents prefer to be told as soon as possible, and together if there are 2 parents. Also it is always best to have the baby present as the child can sometimes feel a stranger or an object rather than a small human being, especially if a label describing a condition is going to be attached to him or her.

Being given inappropriate and out-of-date information at the time of diagnosis is also a common experience of many parents. Sometimes an over negative picture of the condition is given or, at the other extreme, false hopes are raised. Thankfully, the medical profession is becoming more aware of and sensitive to the needs of parents when a diagnosis is given. Unfortunately, however, there are still a number of parents who experience an insensitivity and lack of information when the news is broken. Remember though, that when you are given some news which is a shock and difficult to deal with, your capacity for taking in all what is said is very limited. The right timing of receiving information which is relevant and useful is essential. For some, the time for this after diagnosis comes quicker than for others. This needs to be judged carefully by the professional working with you. However, it is important that you ask more questions when you feel you are ready as you may not want to do this straightaway.

For some parents, a diagnosis is made a while after birth or a diagnosis can never be made at all. The vast majority of these parents will have concerns and worries about their child's development a long time before they are recognised by the medical profession. These parents are often dismissed and labelled as being neurotic. If you are one of these parents, it is important that you keep asking questions about your child and about the help you may be entitled to.

Parents - like their children - are all different but may experience some or all of the following reactions and emotions when they discover their child has a disability. If you have experienced some of these, it may help you to know that you are not alone in having these feelings.

Shock

Shock is often expressed as a physical sensation such as feeling cold, nauseous, as if you are going to faint, or perspiring. Shock is an immediate reaction to some news and it is at this point that it may be particularly difficult to take in information which is given to you.

Disbelief

Not wanting to believe the news or realisation that your child is disabled is a very natural and common reaction. Denial is a way of protecting ourselves and we all do it to some extent. It is only unhealthy to deny such news if this reaction continues for a long while after the diagnosis and if it prevents you from pursuing all the necessary help and support for your child in order for s/he to develop to his or her potential.

Anger

Finding out that your child is disabled is not something that can be changed. Not having a choice or control over the situation can often lead to frustration and anger, which again, is a common and natural emotion to experience. Anger, in small doses, can sometimes be constructive as it can be energising, but sometimes it turns in on itself and leads to depression.

Depression

Depression can express itself through feelings of pessimism and hopelessness and lead to difficulties in eating and sleeping. Crying frequently and losing interest, energy and enthusiasm in life around you are typical signs. If you think you are suffering from depression and recognise some or all of these signs, it is important to seek professional help, from your G.P., health visitor, social services or voluntary agency. The end of this chapter and the next give more details on sources of help and support. You may be offered medication to help your depression, such as anti-depressants. It is your decision whether or not to take them, but if you do, it is also important to express your feelings to a skilled listener and to seek practical and emotional help such as a parent group and services such as day care and/or respite care to give yourself some space.

Grief

Although depression is a serious reaction to the news that your child is disabled and something which needs professional help, remember that feeling a certain amount of sadness and grief is totally understandable and must be expected. These feelings are very similar to those when you have lost someone very close to you. Although you have not lost your child in terms of his or her life, you have lost the child you hoped to have and have to start changing the expectations you have for him or her.

Guilt

Many parents experience a great sense of guilt about having a disabled child. If you can identify with this, you may have blamed yourself - or your partner - for carrying a particular gene or doing something, or not doing something, during pregnancy. You may also feel like you have been punished for something. Remember that in the vast majority of cases, having a disabled child is out of our control and cannot be helped.

Along with feeling guilty, you may also feel like you have let everyone down, i.e. your partner, your family and other children. You may also feel embarrassed to face people and to go out with your child, cutting yourself from friends. Later on in this chapter, there will be more discussion about the reactions and emotions of friends and how to cope with these.

Negative Feelings Towards Your Child

One emotion that is particularly difficult to deal with and which most parents feel terribly guilty about is feeling revolted by the look of their child. Many children who have disabilities of course do not look different; many do, however, and particularly at first, some parents find this hard to deal with and accept. It is important to say that it often takes a while before a bond develops between a child and his or her parent(s). Many parents say that at first their child feels like a stranger to begin with, especially is he or she needs a lot of physical care. It is often only when the young child starts to respond through smiling or making noises other than crying and

13

appears to be more like a real person with his/her own character, that they feel really comfortable being with them.

You may also at times feel over protective towards your disabled child. Again this is a normal reaction and is probably quite instinctive. It does become problematic, however, if being over protective prevents the child developing his or her own independence to the best of his or her ability.
If you have feelings of wanting to harm your child, you must seek help immediately. Help can be obtained from your G.P., social services (emergency social services if it is outside office hours - the number will be under your local council in the telephone directory) or organisations such as Parentline, CRY-SIS and the NSPCC (details at the end of this chapter and in the section on useful addresses.

If you feel like hitting your child, it is always best to leave the room even if you have to leave the child crying. Crying will not harm the child, hitting him or her will. If you feel the need to express your frustration, anger or aggression, hit something else, like a pillow, very hard. In any event, you should always pick up the phone to someone, whether it is a friend, relative, professional or helpline, before you lash out.

How to Cope with Your Reactions and Emotions

Most of the emotions and reactions listed are very negative feelings. Remember that, with time and support, the vast majority of parents do cope. Not only do they cope but they also get great pleasure from their disabled child and find them and witnessing their development extremely rewarding.

The best way of coping with all of these feelings is to talk about them as openly as possible with friends, family, other parents and sympathetic professionals. Let yourself cry and share your anger, guilt and frustration.

Supportive parent groups are run by MENCAP and Contact a Family and other organisations for specific disabilities, such as the Down's Syndrome Association. Phone the national organisation and find out about local groups. Contact a Family also runs groups for parents of children of specific, and sometimes rare, conditions. Their phone number is listed at the end of this chapter, whilst other useful organisations are listed at the end of the book.

It is also important to attempt to continue as normal a life as possible. Going out to see friends, for example, and doing the things you enjoy doing are important ways of preventing the needs of your disabled child, whilst being of primary importance, becoming the only focus for you and your family. Clearly, seeing friends and doing things you enjoy are often easier said than done, especially if you have little practical support and/or you have sole responsibility for the care of your child. Seeking help from statutory (e.g. health or social services) or voluntary agencies may enable you to find the practical and emotional assistance you need.

Finally, it is worth noting that although you may stop feeling saddened and guilty about your child, some of these feelings may return just as you though you were coping well. These feelings will pass as they did before, probably making you feel stronger than ever.

REACTIONS AND EMOTIONS OF PARTNERS

If you have a partner, s/he is likely to experience many of the reactions and emotions already described, but it is not likely to respond in exactly the same way as you. Remember that s/he is a different and unique person!

Whatever you and your partner is feeling, it is always best to try and discuss and share each other's feelings. It may sometimes be hard to understand why your partner feels something if you do not, but it is important to listen to and respect these feelings. Bottling up emotions often results in increased tensions and misunderstandings so talking is vital.

Remember you won't agree on everything to do with your child's disability and how to bring him or her up, something you have most likely discovered in your relationship about other issues. It will sometimes be necessary for you to compromise, therefore, and to try and see your partner's point of view.

It is probably true to say that the relationship between parents is one of the most significant factors in how a family adjusts to a disability and how the disabled child, him or herself, copes. Having a disabled child undoubtedly puts a strain on a relationship but this is not to say that the relationship will fail. The most successful partnerships seem to be where each person is prepared to share his or her feelings, supports the other through difficult times and puts great value on spending quality time together.

If it is not possible for you and your partner to discuss and respect each other's feelings and the tensions and conflicts become too much, it is always best to request help from a skilled professional, such as a counsellor (from Relate, for example) rather than let the issues to go on unresolved. However much you may try and cover up the difficulties in your relationship, children - including disabled children of course - are sensitive to and pick up vibes, and will be affected by them.

If your partner is male and he is your child's father, it may be that he will experience the disability, particularly at first, in a more negative way. Generally speaking, mothers bond more quickly with children and the father may, to begin with, experience feelings of rejection towards the child. Involving him as much as possible in the child's care, appointments with professionals and in the child's general development may help change this initial reaction. In time, and with this involvement, he will most likely

16

become a source of strength, sharing with you the anxieties, challenges and happiness in caring for your child.

REACTIONS AND EMOTIONS OF RELATIVES

Your relatives need to be told very soon that your child is disabled, if a diagnosis is made. It is always best to tell people with your child present, especially if s/he is a baby.

Your relatives will also experience many of the emotions and reactions already described in this chapter. Close relatives such as the child's grandparents are likely to feel a sense of guilt and worry that they have been responsible if there is a genetic problem. It is also possible that they will have old fashioned views about disability and may need up-to-date information and the child's condition and what it may mean, in a practical sense, to care for the child.

Relatives may want to help by babysitting and doing housework, for example, and this may assist them in coping with their feelings and possible guilt.

REACTIONS AND EMOTIONS OF FRIENDS

If you receive a diagnosis when your child is a baby, try and tell your friends about your child's disability as soon as possible. Many parents put this off and it then becomes more and more difficult, sometimes resulting in them avoiding going out with the baby in case someone sees him or her and notices that 'something is wrong'.

You will probably feel relieved once you have told friends about your child's disability. Sometimes, though, friends will feel uncomfortable when you tell them and will not know how to respond. This is because many people are afraid of disability and don't know how to deal with it. Again, if they can see the child/baby as soon as possible, this will reinforce the fact that the child is a child first and foremost, and will make them concentrate less on the disability or condition.

Like relatives, they will often feel better if they can help you out and feel as if they are doing something constructive. So if they are willing to help you, ask them to do something practical and specific, like a bit of shopping or babysitting, which will make them feel more relaxed and able to offer practical support.

REACTIONS AND EMOTIONS OF YOUR DISABLED CHILD'S SIBLINGS.

It is important to tell your other child(ren) about your disabled child as soon as possible. Otherwise, they will pick up vibes from you and the rest of your family, is likely to overhear conversations and worry that something is wrong. Many children fantasize about situations they have sensed and start to believe they are to blame. They, therefore, need both information and reassurance early on.

How much you tell your child(ren), though, clearly depends on how old they are. Children under the age of 3 are still too young to understand details about their sibling's disability or condition. But they can be told you are feeling sad and that his or her sibling needs lots of care and attention. Children this age may present more difficult behaviour in response to this. They may have more tantrums or cling to you or show attention seeking behaviour.

Older children can be told a bit more about their sibling's disability. Use simple terms and do not describe the disability as an illness as this will confuse them. Most children will understand the concept of disability or handicap or the explanation that your disabled child cannot do as much as other children.

Much older siblings like teenagers are likely to respond in much the same way as adults and experience some of the emotions described earlier in this chapter. You need to give them time and space to express these feelings.

Although brothers and sisters will be very significant people in your disabled child's life, it is important to remember two main principles:

i) share your time between all your children. Siblings should have special time with their parents, even if this means organising respite care (e.g. babysitting or time being cared by others in a family or residential setting) for your disabled child;

ii) siblings need to be reassured that it is not their responsibility to take on the care of their disabled sibling when you are no longer around.

Sometimes siblings are teased about their disabled brother or sister, perhaps by other children at school. They are likely to feel upset and angry about this. It is important to be aware of and sensitive to this possibility and to listen to their feelings.

Siblings can be helped in coping with their feelings about having a disabled brother or sister through siblings groups which are sometimes run by voluntary agencies or social services departments, or by involving the class teacher, who may be able to help by initiating a discussion about disability in class, or through children's books on disability.

Like partners, relatives and friends, try and enable your other children to become involved in your disabled child's life and development. You will probably find that although some difficulties may exist, such as jealousy

19

and resentment, overall, siblings will become caring and supportive friends to their disabled brother or sister.

Now read the key points from Chapter 1 overleaf.

KEY POINTS

- You will experience a number of emotions when you discover your child has a disability, such as shock, grief, denial, anger, guilt, and possibly depression and negative feelings towards your child;

- You may not experience all of these emotions and some of them may come and go;

- Your partner, relatives, friends and older children may also experience some of these feelings but they won't react in exactly the same way as you - they are different people - so try and respect their feelings;

- Try and involve your partner, relatives, friends and older children in your disabled child's care and development;

Remember that however bad you feel, you are not alone, as there are others in the same or similar situation. Also it is worth bearing in mind that the vast majority of parents do cope and end up enjoying caring for their disabled child. Meeting other parents through organisations may be very helpful to you.

USEFUL ORGANISATIONS

Contact A Family
170 Tottenham Court Road, London W1P OHA
0171-383 3555

Information and support groups for specific (including rare) conditions.

MENCAP
123 Golden Lane, London EC1Y ORT
0171-253 9433
Information and local groups.

PARENTLINE
National Office: Endway House, The Endway, Hadleigh, Essex SS7 2AN
Administration: 01702 554782

Helpline: 01702 559900
Network of 24 regional telephone helplines for parents under stress, run by trained volunteers who are themselves parents.

CRY-SIS
BM Cry-sis, London WC1 3XX
0171 404 5011

Helpline and support for parents of crying children.

NSPCC (National Society for the Prevention of Cruelty to Children)
42 Curtain Road, London EC2A 3NH
0171 825 2500

NSPCC Child Protection Helpline 0800 800 500

RELATE (MARRIAGE GUIDANCE)
Herbert Gray College, Little Church Street, Rugby CV21 3AP
01788 73241

Runs counselling for couples throughout the country.
For more useful organisations, please see the last section of this book.

2

WHO CAN HELP? WHO DOES WHAT?

When you have a disabled child, you will come into contact with a variety of professionals from health services, social services, education and voluntary agencies, throughout your son or daughter's childhood and early adulthood. This can sometimes feel overwhelming especially if you feel confused about each professional's role, how they can help you and your child, and who employs them. This chapter, therefore, attempts to define clearly and simply the different professionals' roles and how they can help.

You may hear the terms, statutory and voluntary agencies. Statutory services are the ones run by the state under legislation, such as the health service (e.g. NHS and Community Care Act 1990), social services (e.g. The Children Act 1989), education (e.g. the Education Act 1994), housing and so on. Health services are run by trusts and regional health authorities which usually cover different areas from the other services mentioned, which are run by your local council. Voluntary agencies in contrast are run by committees made up of interested volunteers and often employ paid staff to run services, such as play schemes, residential care and so on. They are also pressure groups as they normally work for a particular group in society and contribute to a campaign which aims to improve the quality of life for those people. MENCAP is a good example of a voluntary agency.

Its policies are ultimately governed by a voluntary committee, but it employs numerous paid staff in its national headquarters and in many local organisations throughout the country. It runs services for children and adults with a learning disability and their families and also campaigns for better rights for those people.

Having a disabled child means coming into contact with professionals from the health service from an early stage. Below is a list of the professionals you may encounter and what they do.

HEALTH SERVICE

Health Visitor

Health Visitors are nurses who have had a year's additional training to specialise in working in the community with a broader public health/health promotion role. They officially work with all client groups and ages, although in practice the vast majority of their time is spent working with families of children aged 0 to 5. Most of their role involves advising parents on issues such as feeding, growth and development and immunisations.

Specialist Health Visitor

Not all health authorities employ specialist health visitors. Where they do, they have a particular interest, or specialist training, in both physically and learning disabled children. Apart from the role described above, the specialist health visitor should also be able to offer practical advice on caring for a disabled child and to liaise with other health staff and other agencies to help you obtain all available services. They should also be able to offer you counselling or advice on where you can receive counselling.

G.P (General Practitioner)

The G.P.'s role is to provide health care for your disabled child and your family, either by dealing with any issue him or herself or by referring you to more specialist services. For example, the G.P. may refer your disabled child to specialist services such as a psychologist, physiotherapist, occupational therapist, speech therapist or a consultant paediatrician (see below for definitions).

Consultant Paediatrician

The Consultant Paediatrician is the most senior of a team of doctors specialising in working with children.

Clinical Medical Officer (CMO)

The Clinical Medical Officer is a doctor who is present at child health clinics and who carries out school medicals.

Hospital Doctors and Nurses

A number of titles are used to describe doctors who work in a hospital and distinguish between senior and junior doctors. The following list starts with the most senior and works down:

Consultant
Senior Registrar - Sen. Reg.
Registrar - Reg.
Senior House Officer - SHO
House Officer - HO
Student Doctor or Medical Student

There are also many different types of nurses. Some of the main ones are listed below:

Ward Sister: responsible for the day to day running of a ward and all the nurses working there.
Charge Nurse: the male equivalent of the ward sister.
Registered General Nurse - RGN
Registered Sick Children's Nurse - RSCN
Registered Mental Nurse - RMN
Registered Nurse Mental Handicap - RNMH
Staff Nurse - SN: has completed a period if training in nursing.
Enrolled Nurse - EN: a nurse who has completed a shorter period of training than a staff nurse.
Clinical Nurse Specialist - CNS: works within a specialist area.
Senior Nurse: is in charge of the management of a ward or department. Is sometimes known as the Clinical Nurse Manager or Ward Manager.

You may hear the terms, locum or agency. These terms refer to a temporary member of staff who covers for sickness and/or holidays.

Physiotherapist

A physiotherapist, or physio. for short, helps the child's or adult's bodily co-ordination, muscle tone and motor control, such as learning to walk and sitting up straight, by using a variety of methods such as exercises and massage. The ultimate purpose of physiotherapy is to help the child or adult gain as much independence as possible.

Occupational Therapist (O.T.)

O.T.s are trained to look at self-help and appropriate equipment for children and/or adults, which help them be as independent as possible.

They may teach children with disabilities individual skills such as washing, dressing, feeding and toileting and may be able to help with behaviour problems. A large part of their role is assessing disabled children and adults for adaptations in the home (e.g. a special chair, bath seat) and monitoring them after they have been installed, to ensure the child or adult can live as independently as possible.

Occupational Therapists can be employed by the health service, social services departments and by the housing department.

Clinical Psychologist

Clinical Psychologists are specialists in assessing and treating children and adults with behaviour and/or emotional difficulties. Working with learning disabled children will be part of their training and they will be able to help the child develop effective and adaptive skills in areas such as communication, coping, problem solving and relationships. The Clinical Psychologist will do this by talking at length to the family and other professionals about the problem behaviour and by observing the child/young adult and will then devise a programme or set of guidelines for the family and other professionals (e.g. school staff) to follow when they are with the child.

Incontinence Advisors

Most health authorities have a Continence Advisor. Ask your G.P., Paediatrician or health visitor.

Speech and Language Therapist

Speech and language therapists assess and treat children and adults who have speech, language and hearing difficulties. They help to correct any speech disorders and will advise parents and other professionals, especially school staff, on how they can help the child to improve his or her speech. Unfortunately, most areas have a severe shortage of speech therapists.

Audiologist

An audiologist works with children who have hearing difficulties and will also be able to advise on aids to improve hearing.

Access to any of the above professionals described is usually through your G.P. or other health professional, such as Paediatrician or health visitor.

As your child gets older, you may find services offered by your local social services department very helpful. Some of what they do is listed below:

SOCIAL SERVICES

Social Worker

Social workers assess children or adults and their carers/families, who may need help and support of local services (e.g. respite care), in order to promote their welfare. Social workers have a statutory duty to become involved with a family where it is thought that a child is at risk of harm. They may also be able to offer advice on benefits and be involved in the statementing process (see chapter on education) by writing a social report. Increasingly social services departments have specialist teams of social workers who work only with disabled children and their families.

Occupational Therapist (O.T.)

The role of the O.T. has been described under the health service section. The O.T can also be employed by the social services department. They will either work as part of a team working with both adults or children or they may work as part of a multi-disciplinary social work team for disabled children and their families.

Care Manager

Care managers work with adults who have complex needs (e.g. an adult with a physical or learning disability, mental health problems or the elderly) and is responsible for the co-ordination of services for an individual. Care managers can come from a social work, nursing, occupational therapy or physiotherapy background. Some work for Community Learning Disability or Mental Handicap teams who work with learning disabled adults. They normally start being involved with a young person who has a learning disability around the time of their 16th or 17th birthday, so that the transfer from child care services can be as smooth as possible. Care Managers may be involved in obtaining respite care or long term care away from the family home for learning disabled adults.

Day Care: day nurseries, playgroups and childminding

Social services departments run day nurseries for under 5s who they assess to be in need under the Children Act 1989. Under this legislation, disabled children are automatically considered to be in need and are therefore entitled to some day care. This day care will either be with a day nursery or a childminder who is registered, and therefore approved, by the social services department.

You will need to apply for a day nursery through a social worker, health visitor or at the nursery itself, depending on how your local services work. Lists of registered playgroups and childminders may be obtained from the Registration and Inspection unit of your local social services department.

However, to obtain a free or reduced place with a childminder, again you need to apply through a professional such as your health visitor.

Short-term breaks or respite care

Most social services run some sort of respite care services for disabled children and their families. This will either be a family based service, where your child will stay with another family, who has been thoroughly assessed and approved, for short-breaks (e.g. overnight, weekends occasionally) or will be a residential home. Respite care is usually difficult to obtain as there is so much demand for this type of service, so it is important to ask about this quite early on and be prepared to wait a while.

Register of children with disabilities

Under the Children Act 1989, social services departments have a duty to set up a register of disabled children in their local area. This is so they can plan for future services for children who have disabilities.

Help with transport

Social services departments administer the travel permit for disabled people (including children) and the orange badge scheme for disabled drivers or the carers of disabled children/adults who drive them around on a regular basis. More details about this can be found in chapter 6.

For most of the above services you will not need an allocated social worker as not every family of a disabled child will be able to have one. Your first port of call to gain access to any of these services is, therefore, through a duty social worker who will work in your local social services office. Look up the address and telephone number in your telephone directory. It is always best to ring and find out the time the duty social worker is available and/or to make an appointment

By the time your child is 4 or 5 , you will have more contact with the education services than with any other service. There is more information on education in chapter 4.

EDUCATION

Special Needs Education Department

Most Education Departments of local councils will have a specific special needs education section. You should be able to find this under your local council in the telephone directory. This section will deal with the statementing of children who have special needs or disabilities (a statement is a document that sets out a child's special educational needs and extra help that she or he should get. See chapter 4 for more details on statementing) and will have a list of all the special schools in your area.

Education Psychologist

An education psychologist is a specialist in how children and young people develop and learn. They work closely with teachers and parents as well as the child, to assess and treat a child who may be experiencing difficulties in their learning and/or in their social and emotional well-being at school.

Portage

Portage is a pre-school teaching service which helps parents to teach their baby/child whose development is delayed. Portage Services normally involve a home visitor coming to the home about once a week, deciding with the parents or carer what the baby or child needs to learn and how this should be attained. In some areas Portage is available through social services or health.

Peripatetic teacher

This is a teacher who works in several schools.

You will not necessarily have any contact with voluntary agencies but many parents find the services, information and support that they gain from them invaluable.

VOLUNTARY SECTOR

As discussed at the beginning of this chapter, voluntary agencies are set up to work for specific groups in society, such as Age Concern for the elderly or MIND for those with mental health problems. There are many voluntary organisations for disabled children, some of which are big national agencies with local branches (e.g. MENCAP, ASBAH), and some of which are smaller and are only locally based. Some of these voluntary organisations work for all disabled children (e.g. MENCAP) whilst some are set up for children with a specific disability (e.g. Down's Syndrome Association, National Autistic Society). Contact a Family is a good organisation to contact for unusual or non-specific disabilities.

Most voluntary agencies offer a variety of services, which include the following:

Contact with other parents through support groups-

Telephone or drop-in advice service-

Play schemes, toy libraries, playgroups or baby sitting-

Family-based respite care-

A regular newsletter-

Information about specific disabilities or conditions-

Information about local services for disabled children and welfare benefits and-

General support and advocacy when liaising with benefit agencies and other authorities, such as education, social services, health and housing.

A list of all the main voluntary organisations for disabled children can be found at the end of this book.

Now read the key points from Chapter 2 overleaf.

KEY POINTS

- Help with caring for your disabled child is available from professionals working in statutory services (e.g. health, social services, education) and voluntary organisations.

- Most health professionals can be accessed through your G.P. or health visitor so ask them if you and your child can be referred to specialist services.

- Most services offered by social services, such as respite care, day care and help with equipment and transport can be obtained, in the first instance, through a duty social worker. You can find the number of your local social services office in the telephone directory. Phone first and find out the opening times and/or to make an appointment. Find out if your local social services department has a specialist team for children with disabilities;

- Your disabled child may need to attend a special school or s/he may be able to go to a mainstream school, where extra help may be available. Your child's statement of special education needs will make recommendations. See chapter 4 for more information;

- Voluntary organisations are a good source of information and support. Many organisations have local branches. Use the list at the end of this book or ask your G.P., health visitor or local social services office.

3

FINANCES

Many parents feel guilty or stigmatised about claiming money to look after their child. Remember that benefits are not a privilege or a handout; they are a right and are designed to meet the extra costs incurred when caring for a child with a disability, such as extra clothing, heating and transport. It is therefore very important that you claim every thing you and your child is entitled to.

This chapter outlines the welfare benefits you and your family may be entitled to if you have a disabled child. It also gives information about another source of help - the Family Fund - if your child is severely disabled, and advice about leaving money in a will to a learning disabled son or daughter, a worry of many parents.

WELFARE BENEFITS

Income Support

Income Support is a means-tested benefit to help people who are unemployed and do not qualify for unemployment benefit because they have not paid enough national insurance contributions or work less than 16 hours a week and do not have enough money to live on. You will not qualify for Income Support if you have savings of more than £8000. There are different rates of income support depending on your age: for example, the rate in 1999-2000 (changing in April 2000) for those age 18-24 was £40.70 per week; for those aged 25 or over, the rate was £51.40

On top of the basic rate of income support, premiums may be added for people with additional needs, such as people with children. They are as follows:

- Family Premium - if you have at least one child. In 1999-2000 this was £13.90

- Disabled Child Premium - if you have a child who is getting Disabled Living Allowance for care or mobility at any rate, (see below) or who is registered blind. This premium is not always given automatically, so make sure you claim it if you qualify. The rate in 1999-2000 was £21.90 per week.

- Lone Parent Premium - if you are bringing up children on your own. In 1999-2000 this was £15.75 per week.

- Carer Premium - if your child receives Disability Living Allowance or if you receive Invalid Care Allowance. In 1999-2000 this was £13.95 per week.

There are other premiums for long-term sick or disabled people and for people aged 60 or over.

If you get Income Support, you or anyone you claim for will also get: free prescriptions, free eyesight tests and vouchers to help with the cost of glasses, free school meals, free NHS dental treatment, help with the cost of travelling to hospital for NHS treatment, free milk and vitamins for pregnant women and for children up to 5 years old, and cold weather payments if your benefit includes Disabled Child Premium, or if you have a child under 5.

If you want more information about Income Support:

Call Freeline Social Security on 0800 666555, or get in touch with your local Benefits Agency office (i.e. what used to be called the DSS, the Department of Social Security office).

Disability Living Allowance (DLA)

This benefit is not means-tested, i.e. it is paid to people according to their needs and not their earnings.

Disability Living Allowance is payable in 2 parts: care component and mobility component. Either or both components can be claimed. The care component is paid at three different rates and the mobility component at two. The mobility component can only be paid from the age of 5 years whilst the care component has a lower limit of 3 months. DLA only applies to children and adults under the age of 66. After that, Attendance Allowance applies.

Care Component

If, because of a physical or mental disability, your child needs a lot of looking after or help with personal care, s/he should be entitled to the care component. To qualify, a child must have needed extra help for three months and must be likely to need extra help for a further six months or more. You can claim before the three months are up if you think your child will qualify.

Children or adults not expected to live longer than six months do not have to wait for three months and should be paid the higher rate ot the care component immediately, regardless of the amount of care needed.

Sometimes keeping a diary showing the extra help your child needs can mean the difference between getting DLA or not or between getting different rates. A diary may be helpful if your child's need for attention is unpredictable, or changes from day to day; your child's condition is getting worse; you need to show, for example, times you have had to get up to look after your child in the night and why, and the times you are able to get back to bed; or you want to show your child's need for continual supervision to prevent substantial danger to him or herself or others.

The care component rates for 1999-2000 were:

higher rate	£52.95 per week.
Middle rate	£35.40
lower rate	£14.05 " "

Mobility Component

If a person needs help getting around, s/he may qualify for the mobility component of DLA. A child needs to be at least age 5 before qualifying. People who cannot walk at all, who have severe difficulties in walking or who are deaf and blind should qualify for the higher rate. People who have severe behavioural problems should also qualify for the higher rate, provided that they also get the higher rate of the care component.

Those who do not qualify for the higher mobility rate may be able to get the lower rate if they can walk but need guidance or supervision from someone else when outdoors.

The rates for the mobility component of DLA in 1999-2000 were:

higher £37 p.w.
lower £14.05 "

Claiming DLA

You can obtain a DLA claim pack from your local Benefits Agency or by telephoning the Benefit Enquiry Line on Freephone 0800 882200 or 0800 243355 (minicom) or 0800 220674 in Northern Ireland.

The claim pack is very lengthy and complicated. You are more likely to be successful in your claim if you can find someone to help you with the form. You could ask your health visitor, a social worker (particularly if your social services department has a social work team for children with disabilities), adviser at a local voluntary agency or Citizens Advice Bureau.

If you are not happy with the outcome of your application for DLA, you can ask for a review within three months of the date the decision was sent to you. You can ask for a review at any time if your child's condition changes and you think s/he may be eligible for a different rate of DLA, or if the original decision ignored or misunderstood some relevant fact of your child's case. If you are still not happy after the review, you have the right to appeal to an Independent Disability Appeal Tribunal within three months of the date you received the review decision. If you are appealing, it is advisable to seek expert advice from a Citizens Advice Bureau.

Invalid Care Allowance (ICA)

This is a weekly cash allowance for anyone under the age of 65 who spends at least 35 hours a week looking after someone who gets the higher or middle rate of DLA for personal care. To qualify, you do not have to be related to the person you care for nor live at the same address.

ICA is a taxable allowance but you can still earn up to £50 per week, after deductions, while you are claiming ICA. You cannot get ICA if you are receiving a national insurance benefit such as Widow's Pension or Invalidity Benefit. If you receive Income Support and ICA, the amount of the ICA will be taken off your Income Support. It is still worth claiming both benefits, however, because you will be entitled to the Carer Premium worth £13.95 per week. Make sure you claim the Carer Premium if you qualify for DLA and Income support as it is not always given automatically. ICA, in 1999-2000, was £39.95 per week.

You can get a claim form for ICA (DS700) from your local Benefits Agency or Post Office or by telephoning the Benefit Enquiry Line free on 0800 882200 or 0800 243355 (minicom) or 0800 220674 in Northern Ireland.

Please note that ICA claims can be backdated for 52 weeks as long as the conditions were met. This also applies to the Carer Premium.

Replacement of Family Credit and Disability Working Allowance

Tax credits introduces the Working Families Tax Credit (WFTC)and the Disabled Persons Tax Credit (DPTC).

WFTC is a means tested benefit for families with dependent children where the person works 16 hours+. WFTC will replace Family credit on 5th October 1999.

DPTC will replace Disability Working Allowance, this is similar to WFTC but eligibility is based on disability affecting the applicants ability to work.

Tax Credit will be administered by the Inland Revenue and initially will be paid by them, with Employers starting to make payments in April 2000 (in many cases). However, where the applicant is one of a couple, there will be an option for payment to be made by the Inland Revenue to the partner who is not working or is self employed.

For more information and a claim form (FC1 or FCS1 in Northern Ireland), telephone free on 0800 500222 or contact your local Benefits Agency.

Social Fund

If you are on Income Support and you or someone in you family is disabled or seriously ill you may be able to get a Community Care Grant to pay for certain items which you cannot afford out of your weekly benefit. These may include clothing, bedding, laundry, equipment, minor structural repairs, gas and electricity reconnection charges, redecoration and furnishings, heaters, safety items and fares to visit a close relative in hospital. Any savings over £500 will be deducted from the grant.

It is up to the Benefits Agency whether you get a grant or not. If you apply for a grant you may be turned down or offered a budgeting loan instead. If you accept a loan you will have to pay it back out of your weekly benefit.

For more details ask for Benefits Agency for form SF300.

Fares to Hospital

If you are on Income Support or Family Credit you are entitled to travel costs to and from hospital for NHS treatment when escorting your child. If you are not getting these benefits but are on a low income, you may still be able to get help.

To find out more, ask for leaflet H1 'NHS Hospital Travel Costs' at the hospital or from your local Benefits Agency.

Road Tax Exemption (Vehicle Excise Duty)

If your child gets the higher rate of the mobility component of DLA, you should have been sent a Vehicle Excise Duty exemption form by the DSS automatically.

If you have not received a form, write to the Disability Allowance Unit, Warbreck House, Warbreck Hill, Blackpool, FT2 OTE.

You will not be able to claim exemption from road tax if your child receives only the lower rate of the mobility component of DLA.

Housing Benefit

This is a benefit to help you pay your rent or service charges if you are on Income Support or a low income and have less than £6,000 savings. No help is available towards charges paid to close relatives such as parents. The arrangements must be commercial, for example, with a landlord, housing association or local council.

You need to go to your local council Housing Department for information about claiming Housing Benefit.

Council Tax Benefit

This is financial help from a local council towards your Council Tax bill. If you are on Income Support or a low income you may be able to claim help up to 100% of your bill.

People who are severely mentally disabled may not have to pay Council Tax. Disability reductions are also available if you or a child have a major disability and therefore require a second bathroom, kitchen or other space to meet your needs.

Contact your local council or your local Citizens Advice Bureau for a list of exemptions and reductions and how to apply

Benefits After Age 16.

These include Income Support, Severe Disablement Allowance (SDA), and Disability Living Allowance. These will be covered in chapter 7.

THE FAMILY FUND

The Family Fund is financed by the government and run by the Joseph Rowntree Foundation. The fund is for families who have children under the age of 16 with severe disabilities.

The fund can give lump sums for specific items that arise from the care of the child, such as extra bedding, clothing, a washing machine, tumble dryer, holidays, outings, driving lessons, and play equipment. Although the fund does not means test you, it does assess each application on its own merits, including your social and economic circumstances. After applying, you will be visited by one of the Family Fund's social workers who will make an assessment.

If you do receive financial help from the Family Fund, you can apply again when a new need arises, as long as your child and family still meet the Family Fund criteria. However, the fund is unlikely to help again within 12 months of having made a grant unless there is a particularly urgent need.

To apply, write giving the full name and date of birth of your child and brief details of his/her disability, the types of help you need and whether you have been in touch with the fund before, to:

> The Family Fund
> P.O. Box 50
> York YO1 2ZX

The Family Fund also produces some very useful information sheets on adaptations to housing, bedding and a benefits checklist.

In addition, information is produced on deafness/communication, equipment for daily living, holidays, hyperactivity, transport and a guide to the opportunities available to young disabled people called 'The Next Step'. For other useful publications produced by the Family Fund, please see the section on useful reading at the end of this book.

LEAVING MONEY IN A WILL TO YOUR LEARNING DISABLED SON OR DAUGHTER.

If money is left by will directly to an adult who is not able to deal with it or issue a valid receipt for it because s/he is mentally or learning disabled, a complicated situation may arise where the Court of Protection has to become involved. A receiver appointed by the Court of Protection has power to receive money or property and to deal with it on behalf of someone who is 'mentally disordered' within the meaning of the Mental Health Act 1983 and is unable to manage his/her affairs. Because a receiver would be appointed after your death, you will not have any say over who this person may be or how the property or money left to your son or daughter may be used.

Instead, when it is possible or certain that an adult with learning disabilities will be unable to handle money left to him or her, you should consider setting up a trust for him/her, which will become operational on your death and will last for your son or daughter's lifetime. Trustees, who could be a friend or relative, are appointed to hold the property and/or money and pay it or deal with it on your son or daughter's behalf as you would like.

One great problem, however, in leaving money to a learning disabled son or daughter who is dependent on state benefits, is that once the capital goes beyond £8,000 they will lose their benefit. It is possible to get round this with the help of a solicitor, by setting up a carefully worded trust. Small irregular payments can be paid without affecting Income Support, and can be used as the trustee decides. It could be used for things like holidays or equipment such as a television.

Where children under eighteen are concerned, solicitors will usually recommend that money is left upon a specific form of trust, whether or not the children have learning disabilities, as the law limits a minor's ability to give a valid receipt and to deal with money or property.

For more information, MENCAP have produced a leaflet called 'Leaving money by will to people with learning disabilities' (free of charge). You should also see a Solicitor for more information and advice. MENCAP's legal department can sometimes offer advice to solicitors on this issue.

Now read the key points from Chapter 3.

KEY POINTS

- If you are caring for a disabled child you may be eligible for cash benefits. Make sure you are claiming all you're entitled to by going through this list:

  - Disability Living Allowance (DLA)
  - Invalid Care Allowance (ICA)
  - Road Tax Exemption
  - Fares to hospital
  - Family Credit/Working Families Tax Credit
  - Income Support
  - Social Fund
  - Housing Benefit
  - Council Tax Benefit
  - Further benefits at age 16:

  Income Support
  Severe Disablement Allowance
  Disability Working Allowance/Disabled Persons Tax Credit.

- The Family Fund is a good source of financial help for specific items to do with the care of your child, if s/he is under age 16 and has a severe physical and/or learning disability.

- If you want to leave money or property to your son or daughter who is learning disabled when s/he is over 18 years old, it is best to set up a trust for him or her and appoint a trustee rather than the Court of Protection becoming involved.

USEFUL ORGANISATIONS

Your local Citizens Advice Bureau will be able to help you with benefits and filling out forms. Look them up in your telephone directory to find out the opening times and if it is possible to make an appointment.

The Disability Alliance runs an advice line on Monday and Tuesday between 2pm and 4 pm and between 10.30 am to 12.30 pm on Thursdays.

The number is 0171 247 8763.

The Disability Alliance also produces a 'Disability Rights Handbook' which covers benefits available to people with disabilities and their families.

Disability Alliance
Universal House
88-94 Wentworth Street
London E1 7SA
0171 247 8776

The Family Fund
P.O. Box 50
York YO1 1UY
01904 621115

MENCAP
123 Golden Lane
London EC1Y ORT
0171-253 9433

Department of Social Security

Benefit Enquiry Line for people with disabilities and their carers: 0800 882200 (freephone).

General benefit enquiries:

English	0800 666555(freephone)	
Chinese	0800 252451	"
Urdu	0800 289188	"
Punjabi	0800 521360	"

4

EDUCATION

Your child's education will undoubtedly play an extremely important part in his/her life, as not only will s/he be spending many hours a week in school for many years, but it is how s/he gets on at school that will determine very much how s/he is out of school. It is therefore important that you know as much as possible about the options open to your son or daughter so that s/he is happy at school and has his or her potential developed to the full.

This chapter outlines some of the options for pre-school education, and then discusses the formal assessment of children with disabilities and/or special needs, and the document which often follows an assessment, which is called a statement or the process of statementing. Other education jargon, such as the Code of Practice under the Education Act 1996 will be explained as well as a brief exploration of the debate between integration and segregation of disabled children in the education system.

PRE-SCHOOL EDUCATION

Whatever the extent of your child's disability, s/he will be helped by some pre-school education to prepare him or her for full-time school and to help him or her develop to his or her full potential. Opportunities for pre-school learning for your child include portage, playgroups, day nurseries and nursery classes.

Portage

Portage is a home-based learning programme which can commence as early as when your child is only a few months old. Portage, which has already been described in chapter 2, is a very important source of pre-school education and can be invaluable in teaching your child new skills. Apart from asking your G.P., Paediatrician or health visitor about portage, you could contact the National Portage Association for details of local schemes (see the end of this chapter for the address and telephone number).

Playgroups

Playgroups and opportunity groups can help your child develop socially by mixing with other young children and through play. Ask your health visitor and/or the Pre-school Playgroups Association (address at end of chapter) for playgroups which are available in your area.

Day Nurseries

Day nurseries can be run by social services or by private individuals or groups. Remember that under the Children Act 1989, your child if s/he is disabled is a "child in need" and consequently, has a right to some day care up to the age of 5. Contact your local Social Services Office for more information and advice.

Nursery Classes

Unfortunately there are few nursery class places throughout the country.

However, if your child is recognised as having special educational needs from an early age, s/he may be entitled to high priority for a nursery place. Ask your Local Education Authority about the schools you should approach.

Peripatetic Teachers

It also may be possible for the Local Education Authority to arrange a Peripatetic Teacher to visit you and your child at home, depending on whether this service is available in your area. Some of these teachers may specialise in hearing or visual impairments, or both.

ASSESSMENT OF SPECIAL EDUCATIONAL NEEDS

Children have their special education needs assessed if they have learning difficulties and need special help. A child has learning difficulties if s/he finds it much harder to learn than most children of the same age, or if s/he has a disability which makes it difficult to use the ordinary education facilities in the area.

Pre-school

If your child has not received a specific diagnosis or recognition from the medical profession that his or her development is delayed, and s/he has not yet started school and you are concerned that s/he may need specialist help, you need to talk to a professional such as a doctor, health visitor etc. Or you can talk to the Local Education Authority (LEA) directly instead for advice. The phone number of the LEA will be in your telephone directory under your local council. You can ask your LEA to make a statutory assessment of his or her special educational needs. The LEA must then make a statutory assessment, unless they decide it is unnecessary.

If your child has been diagnosed as having a condition or disability from a young age, a health professional will probably refer him or her directly to the LEA, after consulting you. They will discuss his or her needs with you and look at how best s/he may be helped. The LEA will then decide whether it is necessary to make a statutory assessment.

At School

If your child has already started school and you are concerned that s/he has learning difficulties, you need to talk to your child's teacher or headteacher. At the school there will be someone who has special responsibility for children with special educational needs - the Special Needs Co-ordinator - who you then need to talk to.

Under the Education Act 1996, schools must publish information about their policies for children with special educational needs (SEN) and have regard to what's called a Code of Practice on the Identification and Assessment of SEN. Stages within the Code of Practice are followed before making a statutory assessment of your child's special educational needs. The Code of Practice is described below.

Code of Practice

The Code recommends that schools should deal with a child's needs step-by-step or in stages. Your child will only move from one step to another if it is seen as necessary. These steps or stages are as follows:

Stage One

Your child's teacher should record any concerns about your child's learning difficulty and should speak to you about them. A full discussion of your child's needs, and any relevant history of your child's difficulties, should take place at this stage.

Stage Two

The teacher responsible for special educational needs should talk to you and your child's other teachers and should draw up an individual education plan. This plan sets targets for your child to achieve and a date for a review of his or her progress. The school may ask you to work with your child and to help him or her at home.

Stage Three

At this stage, the school is likely to look for some specialist help or advice from outside the school, such as from an Educational Psychologist or Specialist Teacher. A new individual education plan will be drawn up. You will be kept informed about your child's progress and invited to all review meetings. If your child is not making enough progress, the Headteacher will decide whether to ask the LEA to make a statutory assessment.

Throughout all the stages, you have a right to take part in decisions about your child's education. Your views are very important.

The Statutory Assessment

This is a very detailed examination of what your child's special educational needs are and all the special help s/he may need. Your views are very important and you should be involved in the whole process.

If the LEA decide to make a statutory assessment of your child, they need to tell you within 6 weeks. Sometimes the LEA will decide that your child's needs can be met in his or her present school and do not make a statutory assessment. If you disagree with this you have a right to appeal to the Special Educational Needs Tribunal.

When a statutory assessment takes place, detailed information is collected from your child's school, his or her doctor, an Education Psychologist and most importantly , you, his or her parent(s). You have an essential part to play because you know your child better then anyone else.

The LEA should give you information about the different types of special help that ordinary and special schools in your area can offer. You can then visit some of these schools to decide which you might like your child to attend.

You may feel that you want independent advice when your child's needs are being assessed and discussed. To help you, you are entitled to what's called a Named Person. This is someone who may come from a voluntary organisation, or a parents' support group or be a professional, friend or relative. They should be able to give you advice and information as well as emotional support. Ask your LEA about the Named Persons.

After the assessment is complete, a decision will be made by the LEA whether to make a statement of special educational needs for your child. The LEA should let you know this within 12 weeks of starting the assessment.

STATEMENTS OF SPECIAL EDUCATIONAL NEEDS

A statement of special educational needs is a document that sets out your child's needs and all the special help s/he should have.

A statement of special educational needs is in 6 parts:

Part One: gives your own and your child's name and address and other details.

Part Two: gives details of all your child's learning difficulties and disabilities as identified by the LEA during the assessment.

Part Three: describes all the special help that the LEA think your child should get to meet the needs set out in Part Two; the long-term objectives to be achieved by that special help; and the arrangements to be made for setting short-term targets and regularly reviewing your child's progress towards those targets.

Part Four: tells you about the school where your child will go to get the special help set out in Part three, or the arrangements for education to be made otherwise than at school.

Part Five: describes any non-educational needs your child has, such as transport to school.

Part Six: describes how your child will get the help described in Part five.

Normally it is the Principal Education Psychologist in your area who will prepare the final statement but views should be sought from professionals involved with your child as well as you, the parents. The professionals consulted are likely to include health professionals such as your G.P., Consultant, Physiotherapist, Occupational Therapist, a Social Worker and teaching staff.

Before the LEA sends you the final statement, they will send you a 'proposed statement'. This includes all parts except part 4. With this the LEA will then send you a letter telling you how you can give your views on the proposed statement before it is finalised.

The LEA will also send you details of state ordinary schools and state special schools in your area. You have a right to express a preference for which state school you want your child to go to. However, the LEA must agree with your preference as long as:

(i)   the school you choose is suitable for your child's age, ability and special educational needs;

(ii)   your child's presence there will not affect the education of other children already at the school; and

(iii)   placing your child in the school will be an efficient use of the LEA's resources.

Clearly then, it is quite easy for the LEA to argue against your preference if they see fit. It is important therefore for you to collect as much evidence as possible to demonstrate that your child would be better off in a particular school. The Advisory Centre for Education (see address at the end of this chapter) can offer advice and support to parents whose children are going through the statementing process. Other useful organisations are listed both at the end of this chapter and the book.

After the LEA have sent you the proposed statement, you have 15 days to reply to comment and say which school you would like your child to attend. You can ask for a meeting with the LEA to discuss the proposed statement after which you have another 15 days to send in more comments or request another meeting. Usually the LEA should make the final statement within 8 weeks of the proposed statement.

If you disagree with what is in the statement, you should ask an officer at your LEA for an explanation. If you are still not happy, you have a right to appeal to the Special Educational Needs Tribunal against the contents of part 2, 3 or 4 of the statement. There is more about the Tribunal and what to do if you disagree, in chapter 8.

Once the statement is in place, it must be reviewed at least once a year. The school will do this by holding a review, to which you will be invited to attend. This annual review may lead to changes to your child's statement if his or her needs have changed, the LEA have decided that different kinds of extra help are necessary or if your child has to move to a different school. You will be asked for your views before changes are made.

A child's statement may last for all of his or her school life or just part of it, depending on his or her needs and progress. These will be discussed at reviews.

SEGREGATION versus INTEGRATION IN EDUCATION

The arguments for and against disabled children being educated in mainstream (ordinary) schools or in special schools have been debated fiercely by parents and educationalists over many years.

Special school education means segregated education. Special schools are often a long way from a child's home and therefore separated from his or her local community and peers. Once the child has reached the age of 19, s/he will need, in most cases, to return to his or her local community, from which s/he has been separated for many years. Special schools in the main will emphasise the learning of social skills and independent living skills rather than academic achievement.

However, special schools are favoured by many people because it is at these schools that disabled children have greater access to the services they need, such as physiotherapy, speech therapy and occupational therapy. They will also have specialised teaching equipment and specially trained teachers.

Sometimes when disabled children attend ordinary mainstream schools, they can be over-protected or treated as special because of their disability. This will depend on the school and how the issues of disability and integration are approached by the teaching staff and the ethos of the establishment. However, if this type of treatment of a disabled child does go on, the school is not equipping him or her for independence. Some parents fear the teasing or bullying their child may be subjected to in a mainstream school, or that their child will not be able to keep up with the others.

Other parents and educationalists believe that integration is the answer to equal educational and social opportunities to children who have special educational needs. Attending a mainstream school, it is argued, means that disabled children can grow up within a 'real life' community, can develop out-of-school relationships in his or her local area, will do better academically and will also help those non-disabled children understand the concept of disability and view it more positively.

In many areas, though, both special schools and mainstream schools are pursuing integration policies, by mixing classes from different schools on a regular basis and by having a special unit attached to a mainstream school, for example. It is important for you to be aware of what's available in your local area, so ask your LEA for information as early as possible.

KEY POINTS

- Pre-school education, such as Portage, playgroups, day nurseries and/or nursery classes, is important for your child. Ask your G.P., health visitor or other professional.

- Special educational needs means having learning difficulties and needing extra help at school.

- If your child needs his or her special educational needs assessed before s/he is 5, this will be started by a health professional or yourself asking the Local Education Authority (LEA). If your child is assessed whilst s/he is already at school, Stages 1 to 3 of the Code of Practice will be followed before a statutory assessment starts.

After the assessment, your child may be statemented. A statement is a document that sets out your child's needs and all the special help s/he should have.

If you disagree with any actions of the LEA, you should talk to them or your child's school first. If you are still unhappy, you can appeal to the Special Educational Needs Tribunal. There is more about this in chapter 8.

There are many arguments for and against educating disabled children in special or mainstream schools. In the end, what's decided for your child will be based on your views and the views of the LEA about your child's needs. As far as possible, your child's own views and wishes should be taken into account. Find out all the options as early as possible. Some of the organisations listed below may be able to help.

USEFUL ORGANISATIONS

Advisory Centre for Education (ACE)
1b Aberdeen Studios
22 Highbury Grove
London N5 2EA
0171-354 8321

Open 2-5pm. Produces a Special Education Handbook.

Independent Panel for Special Education Advice (IPSEA)
22 Warren Hill Road
Woodbridge
Suffolk IP12 4DU
01394 382814

Educational psychologists and other professionals with a knowledge of special needs who give direct support to parents and children on a voluntary basis.

The Integration Alliance
34a Datforne Road
Tooting
London SW17 8TZ

Can advise parents on all aspects of integration and produces some useful publications and a newsletter.

Centre for Studies on Integration in Education
415 Edgware Road
London NW2 6NB
0181 452 8642

Information available on the process of assessment and statements, how to appeal against the final statement and reviews.

Network 81
1-7 Woodfield Terrace
Chapel Hill
Stansted
Essex CM24 8AJ
01279 647415 (helpline)

Gives advice on education assessments and statementing.

National Portage Association
4 Clifton Road
Winchester
Hants
01962 860148

Pre-school Playgroups Association
61-63 Kings Cross Road
London WC1X 9LL
0171 833 0991
Helpline: 0171 837 5513

5

BREAKS AND HOLIDAYS

We all need breaks from our everyday routine, whether this is working full-time or caring for someone, or both. Having a breathing space from caring for a disabled child is no exception so try not to feel guilty about it. To make sure you can care for your child as best as you can, you will need time to yourself, with your partner and your other children. Remember too that your disabled child is likely to enjoy the opportunity of doing new things with other children and adults and will probably learn much from the experience. Breaks away with your child are also important and there are now many organisations which can help you plan a holiday with your disabled child.

This chapter outlines some of the possibilities for short-term breaks or respite care, such as family based schemes, playschemes or residential care, and holidays, and lists some organisations which may be of use to you.

RESPITE CARE OR SHORT-TERM BREAKS

Respite care or the newer term - short-term breaks - is often used to describe the situation when a child goes away from the family home overnight to give his or her parent/carer a break. This is misleading as respite care or short-term breaks can also apply to care given to a child in his or her own home whilst the parent/carer goes out, and to short-term breaks during the day, such as playschemes.

Many parents find it very hard to part with their child even when they really need the break, and for a relatively short space of time. You may feel like this and guilty about leaving the care of your child in the hands of someone else who isn't a member of your family or a close friend. This is understandable but can be overcome by planning respite care so that you and your child can get to know someone over a space of time before you leave them in charge of your child. Because respite care may be needed in an emergency - if you were taken ill, for example, and there was no one else to care for your child - is it important for you to check out the respite care possibilities at an early stage before any crisis may occur.

Some of the different types of respite care or short-term breaks are listed and described below.

Family Based Respite Care

Family based respite care schemes are usually run by local voluntary agencies or by social services departments. They assess, recruit, train and monitor single people or families who are able to look after a disabled child in their home on a regular basis, like 1 night a fortnight, a weekend per month, or sometimes longer spells like a week or a fortnight on occasions (e.g. once/twice a year) so the parent(s) can go away.

The procedure for recruiting, assessing and approving carers is very thorough and governed by Children Act 1989 guidelines, and is very similar to the procedure for recruiting foster parents. So you can rest assured from the start that the carer matched to your child is as suitable and capable as possible. Remember too that the person, and any other adult in the same household, would have been checked against Police and social services records. Although this, unfortunately, does not guarantee that the person would not abuse your child in any way, it makes it much less likely.

The scheme which recruits carers for a disabled child will have information about you and your child, what s/he is like, what his or her disabilities are and what his or her likes and dislikes are. They will then match you and your child with a carer they judge to be suitable for your child. They will try and match racial, cultural and religious backgrounds as far as possible. It is then usual for you and your child to meet with the prospective carer and his or her own family on several occasions, at your home and the carer's home, to get to know each other. Only after a few meetings will it be possible for your child to stay overnight at the carer's home.

Family based respite care does not always have to mean overnight care though. Many carers are willing and able to take care of children during the day during the week on occasions (during the school holidays occasionally, for example) or sometimes at the weekend. This can normally be negotiated with the carer and who ever is running the scheme.

Family based respite care schemes tend to work well for both parents and children. Consequently, this means that the schemes that do exist are over-stretched, resulting in long waiting lists. Try and find out what's available in your local area at an early stage, by asking your social services department or voluntary agency.

Residential Respite Care

Residential respite care units for disabled children are run by health, social services or voluntary agencies. They offer overnight care for your child on an emergency or regular basis, if you meet certain criteria which varies depending on the unit. If you are able to plan your child's first stay, it is best to visit the unit with your child to meet some of the staff and look around the facilities. This will mean that parting from your child and seeing your child go away from home will be much easier for you both.

You can find out about what residential respite care is available by asking your health professional, social services department or voluntary agency. It is worth noting that it is not always easy to obtain such care - you need to demonstrate the importance of it for both you and your child. Getting support from a sympathetic professional may also be helpful.

Play schemes and After School Clubs

Play schemes for the school holidays and after school clubs are normally run by the leisure department of your local council, although some are also run by voluntary agencies. They are normally based in schools and offer play activities and outings in a relaxed but supervised environment.

Your child may be able to join the play schemes and clubs run for non-disabled children, depending on what his or her needs are. Special schemes and clubs are also run for disabled children. Ask your leisure department or local voluntary organisation for more information.

Respite Care or Short-term Breaks in Your Home

Many parents feel guilty about taking up respite care opportunities as it feels like they are sending their child away from home. First, many children enjoy this break themselves and learn new things and meet new people whilst away and second, there may also be opportunities for respite care in your home meaning that your child can stay at home whilst you go out.

This type of respite care, however, is not normally for overnights. Such breaks will usually be for care during the day, such as 2-4 hours, to give you time to go shopping, see some friends, or simply spend some time alone or with your partner.

One of the main national organisations offering this type of care is the Crossroads Care Attendant Schemes across the country, and they employ carers who go into families once a week for 4 hours or twice a week for 2 hours. Most families receive a maximum of 4 hours per week but this depends on their needs and circumstances. Carers work all hours so it is possible to have help at weekends and evenings as well as during the day. Crossroads carers work with children and people of all ages and all disabilities.

Some local Crossroads Care Attendant Schemes also offer an occasional night sitting service if your sleep is often interrupted.

Some areas may not have a Crossroads Care Attendant Scheme but will have a similar scheme which works under a different name. Ask the Crossroads Care Attendant national organisation (address at the end of this chapter) or your local social services department, health professional or voluntary organisation to see if you have a local scheme.

HOLIDAYS

Having a disabled child should not mean that you cannot go away. There are many organisations that can help you plan a holiday with your child or who can organise an independent trip for him or her if s/he is old enough.

The following organisations publish information about holidays for the disabled including family holidays, activity holidays and holidays for unaccompanied disabled children and adults.

HOLIDAY CARE SERVICE
2nd Floor
Imperial Building
Victoria Road
Horley
Surrey RH6 7PZ
01293 774535

MENCAP HOLIDAY SERVICES
119 Drake Street
Rochdale
Greater Manchester OL16 1PZ
01706 54111
As well as providing information on holidays, it can also organise holidays and can provide volunteers to accompany disabled children, young people and adults.

RADAR (Royal Association for Disability and Rehabilitation)
12 City Forum
250 City Road
London EC1V 8AF
0171 250 3222

The following organisations can provide holidays and holiday accommodation for disabled children and their families. This is only a small selection of the full list, which can be obtained from RADAR.

BREAK
20 Hooks Hill Road
Sheringham
Norfolk NR26 8NL
01263 823170

Specialises in holidays for multiply disabled children and adults, individuals, groups and those unaccompanied by parents or staff.

ACROSS TRUST
Bridge House
70-72 Bridge Road
East Molesey
Surrey KT8 9HF
0181 783 1355

Organises holidays for disabled people of all ages across Europe in fully equipped Jumbulances.

THE CALVERT TRUST

KEILDER
Keilder Water
Hexham
Northumberland NE48 1BS
01434 250232

KESWICK
Little Crosthwaite
Keswick
Cumbria CA12 4QD
017687 72254

EXMOOR
Wislandpound Farm
Kentisbury
North Devon EX31 4SJ
01598 763221

The Calvert Trust in Northumberland, Cumbria and Devon have purpose built centres for disabled people and their families offering a wide range of sports and recreational activities.

MOBILITY INTERNATIONAL
228 Borough High Street
London SE1 1JX
0171 403 5688

Offers a variety of holidays in the U.K. and abroad for physically disabled young adults.

AFASIC (Association for All Speech Impaired Children)
347 Central Markets
Smithfield
London EC1A 9NH
0171 236 3632

Organises activity holidays for children and young people who have speech and language disorders.

NATIONAL DEAF-BLIND LEAGUE
18 Rainbow Court
Paston Ridings
Peterborough
Cambs PE4 7UP
01733 573511

Organises walking trips and trips in the UK and abroad throughout the year.

BRITISH DIABETIC ASSOCIATION
Youth and Family Services
10 Queen Anne Street
London W1M OBD
0171 323 1531

Offers subsidised activity holidays for members between the ages of 5 and 18 years.

FINANCING HOLIDAYS

Social Services

Disabled children and their families may be able to obtain a small grant from their social services department towards a holiday. The criteria for receiving some funding will vary from one council to another, but many means test and/or will only give money to a family every few years.

Charitable Organisations

THE FAMILY FUND
PO Box 50
York YO1 2ZX

To receive funding, there must be a severely disabled child under the age of 16 in the family. Grants vary in size and can be used towards family holidays with or without the disabled child.

THE FAMILY HOLIDAY ASSOCIATION
Hertford Lodge
East End Road
Finchley

London N3 3QE
0181 349 4044/4047

The Family Holiday Association provides grants for families for one week's holiday of their choice. The family must be referred to the Association by a Social Worker.

PEARSON'S HOLIDAY FUND
Box 123
Bishops Waltham
Hants SO32 1ZE
01489 893260

Funds children aged 4-17 whilst on holiday in the U.K. The fund only deals with the referrer, i.e. the doctor, social worker, health visitor etc, rather than the family.

THE NATIONAL HOLIDAY FUND FOR SICK AND DISABLED CHILDREN
Suite 1
Princess House
1-2 Princess Parade
New Road
Dagenham
Essex RM10 9LS
0181 595 9624

Provides holidays at selected venues throughout the world for chronically or terminally ill children, and physically disabled children between 8 and 18 years.

More information on financing holidays can be obtained from RADAR and the Holiday Care Service. See section on useful reading for more details.

Now read the key points from chapter five.

KEY POINTS

- You may feel guilty about needing a break from your child. This is perfectly understandable but remember that we all need breaks from our everyday routine and caring responsibilities.

- Respite care or short term breaks does covers a variety of possibilities: family based schemes, residential respite care, playschemes, after schoolclubs and care within the home whilst you go out.

- It is not always easy to obtain respite care, so find out about opportunities in your local area from an early stage. It is also always best to plan respite care and meet the person or people who will be caring for your child, so try and apply for respite care before any sort of crisis occurs.

- Having a holiday with your disabled child is also important. There are many organisations which can help you do this, which are listed above. Holidays can also be arranged for your child to go away on his or her own, if s/he is old enough.

USEFUL ORGANISATIONS

CROSSROADS CARE ATTENDANT SCHEMES
10 Regent Place
Rugby
Warwickshire
CV21 2PN
01799 573653

CROSSROADS (SCOTLAND) CARE ATTENDANT SCHEMES LTD
4th floor, 24 George Square
Glasgow G2 1EG
0141 226 3793

SHARED CARE UK (Association to promote family based short-term care)
The Norah Fry Research Centre
3 Priory Road
Bristol BS8 1TX
01272 467230/238137

HOLIDAY CARE SERVICE
2nd Floor
Imperial Building
Victoria Road
Horley
Surrey RH6 7PZ
01293 774535

RADAR
12 City Forum

250 City Road
London EC1V 8AF
0171 250 3222

MENCAP HOLIDAY SERVICES
119 Drake Street
Rochdale
Greater Manchester
OL16 1PZ
01706 54111

6

TRANSPORT AND EQUIPMENT

Help with transport and equipment for your disabled child is designed to make life a little easier for both you and your son or daughter, and can assist both with getting around and encouraging independence. It is best to know what the options are, therefore, which this chapter aims to do by outlining some of the main sources of help with transport and equipment. For more detailed advice about equipment to help your child be as independent as possible, both inside and outside the home, it is advisable to talk to an Occupational Therapist, who can be found in the health service or social services.

FINANCIAL HELP WITH TRANSPORT

Welfare Benefits

This has been dealt with in chapter 3 and covers the following areas relevant to this section:
(i)   fares to hospital
(ii) road tax exemption
(iii) mobility component of the Disabled Living Allowance (DLA)
(iv) social fund

Use this list to make sure you are getting everything you and your child are entitled to.

Family Fund

To receive any help from the Family Fund a family must have a severely disabled child under the age of 16. Please see chapter 3 for more details. To help with transport costs, a child must only be receiving the lower rate of the mobility component of DLA. The Family Fund sometimes agrees to pay for driving lessons for parents.

HELP WITH CAR USE

Buying a Car - Motability

Motability is both a private company and registered charity, which receives a government grant to cover its administrative costs. It helps disabled people or the families of diabled children, who receive the higher rate of the mobility component of DLA, to lease a new car or to buy a new or second-hand car or a powered wheelchair on hire purchase.

For more details of the scheme, contact Motability direct. The address and telephone number is listed at the end of this chapter.

Parking - the Orange Badge Scheme

An orange badge enables disabled people as drivers or passengers or the parents of disabled children to park on a yellow line for up to 2 hours (as long as they are not causing an obstruction) in England and Wales, and without a time limit in Scotland and park without charge or time limit on parking meters. This does not apply in central London.

To qualify, you need to show that you or your child has a permanent and substantial disability which causes very considerable difficulty in walking, which has to be verified by your G.P. or Consultant, or be in receipt of the higher rate of the mobility component of the Disability Living Allowance.

To obtain an orange badge, you need to apply to your local social services office.

PUBLIC TRANSPORT

Travel Permits for Buses and Trains

Many local councils offer travel permits for children and young people who are disabled and over the age of 5. The criteria and availability will vary from one council to another but generally, being in receipt of the higher rate of mobility component of DLA is enough to qualify automatically. If your child does not receive this, your child's G.P. will probably be asked for information to support the application. Ask your local social services office for more details.

Taxicards

A number of local councils offer concessions on the cost of taxi fares. Again, this will vary from one council to another. The critera will be similar to that of the Orange Badge and the travel permit. Ask your local social services office for more details.

COMMUNITY TRANSPORT SCHEMES

Some areas offer cheap transport for people with mobility problems. The names and details of the schemes will vary from one area to another. Ask your local voluntary agency for the disabled or Citizens Advice Bureau for more information.

More information about how you can be helped with transport can be found in leaflets and publications which are listed in the 'Useful Reading' section of this book.

EQUIPMENT

Generally, it is very important that your child has a proper assessment for any equipment s/he needs, by a qualified professional such as an Occupational Therapist or Physiotherapist through social services or the hospital s/he attends.

Buggies and Wheelchairs

If your child has serious problems with walking and is over 2 1/2 years old, you should be able to get him or her a buggy or wheelchair from your local Wheelchair Centre. In Scotland and Wales these are called Artificial Limb and Appliance Centres. In Northern Ireland they are called Prosthetic and Orthotic Aids Centres.

If your child is under 2 1/2 years old, has serious difficulties with walking amd has special seating needs, s/he may still be able to get this help.

Ask your child's GP, hospital specialist, Occupational Therapist to refer your child to the Wheelchair Centre.

Nappies and Incontinence Aids

Once a child is over the age of infancy but is still incontinent as a result of a disability, your local health authority can provide a supply of incontinence aids. These include disposable nappies and pads, bed pads and plastic pants.

Ask your G.P, Community Paediatrician, Health Visitor or School Nurse for advice.

Adaptations to Housing

If your child has a physical disability, it may be necessary to adapt your accommodation. It is advisable to plan ahead as early as possible because it takes a long time to find out what adaptations are necessary and possible and how they will be financed.

It is sometimes possible to receive financial help for adaptations under the Disabled Facilities Grants from your local council. The schemes vary from one area to another, but are always means-tested, so you need to check with your local council what can be offered.

As a first step, you need to talk to an Occupational Therapist at your Social Services Department.

Further information can be obtained from RADAR.

Now read the key points from Chapter 6.

KEY POINTS

- For financial help with transport, you may be entitled to one of the following benefits: social fund help, fares to hospital, mobility component of the DLA, road tax exemption or help from the Family Fund.

- If your child has problems with his or her mobility, you may be eligible for help in obtaining a car through the motability scheme, orange badge for concessions in parking, a travel permit for your child and/or a taxicard.

- Help with equipment such as wheelchairs and other adaptations to your house may be obtained through an Occupational Therapist in the first instance.

USEFUL ORGANISATIONS

MOTABILITY
Gate House
West Gate
Harlow
Essex CM20 1HR
01279 635999
Customer Service Helpline: 01279 635666

RADAR
12 City Forum
250 City Road
London EC1V 8AF
0171 250 3222

DISABLED LIVING FOUNDATION
380-384 Harrow Road
London W9 2HU
0171 289 6111

Gives advice about equipment and all aspects of disabled living.

EQUIPMENT FOR THE DISABLED
Mary Marlborough Lodge
Nuffield Orthopaedic Centre
Headington
Oxfordshire OX3 7LD
01865 750103

7

TOWARDS ADULTHOOD

The transition from childhood to adulthood is a period of change for all young people and their families, and being a disabled young person is no exception to this rule.

It is during the teenage years that services change for a disabled young person, future opportunities for education, training, work and living need to be looked into, new welfare benefits become available and the young person becomes independent, not least in the area of sexuality and relationships. This period can be a difficult time for parents, who may still feel very protective towards their son or daughter and can find it hard to accept that s/he is growing up and growing away, especially if s/he is disabled and is, in some ways, still dependent. All these issues will be addressed in this chapter.

WELFARE BENEFITS AT AGE 16

Once a disabled young person reaches the age of 16, s/he can claim benefits, regardless of his or her parents' income or savings. There are three main benefits for the over 16s, who are disabled: Severe Disablement Allowance (SDA), Disability Living Allowance (DWA) and Income

Support. Although a person's income support is reduced by the amount they are receiving in other benefits, such as SDA, it is still worth applying for both Income Support and SDA because s/he will be entitled to the disability premium of Income Support if certain conditions apply. These benefits and their conditions are outlined below.

Severe Disablement Allowance (SDA)

Severe Disablement Allowance provides a basic income for those who are unable to work because of a disability (even if they are at school or college for less than 21 hours a week or in special education). SDA was £54.40 in 1999-2000. If your son or daughter receives SDA, Disability Living Allowance (DLA), or is registered blind, s/he should also claim Income Support.

To apply for SDA, ask for form N1252 from your local Benefits Agency (Social Security) office or telephone the Benefit Enquiry line free on 0800 882200 or 0800 243355 (minicom).

Income Support

Income Support can be claimed on its own or to "top up" SDA. If SDA is received, the "top up ", i.e. the disability premium, is about £18.45 per week, so it is worth claiming to get this much extra each week. Anyone receiving DLA (Care) at the higher or middle rate or who is registered blind, automatically qualifies for the disability premium.

Young people receiving Income Support who have extra needs caused by their disability, such as extra clothing, bedding or laundry equipment, may apply to the Social Fund for a Community Care Grant, although any savings of £500 or more will be deducted from the grant.

Remember that SDA and Income Support may be claimed while still at school or in further education. Parents should note, however, that if your son or daughter applies for Income Support in his or her own right, you will lose your Child Benefit and premiums for having dependent children, such as Lone Parent premium. You will also have to sign on for work unless you are getting Invalid Care Allowance.

Disability Working Allowance (DWA)and the Disabled Persons Tax Credit (DPTC)

This was a benefit for people ages 16 and over introduced in 1992. This is being replaced by the Disabled Persons Tax Credit (DPTC) in 1999. For more details on how this will work, please see Chapter 3.

Housing Benefit

People aged 16 or over with less than £16,000 savings who pay rent or service charges where they live may be able to get Housing Benefit. Please note that no help is available towards charges paid to close relatives, such as parents. The arrangements must be 'commercial', for example with a landlord, housing association or local council.

To claim housing benefit apply to your local council housing department for a claim form.

EDUCATION AND TRAINING

When your child/young person reaches the age of 14, a reassessment of his or her special educational needs must be made. This should include a 'Transition Plan' which aims to co-ordinate plans for the young person's transition from child to adult services and should include an assessment by the Social Services Department of needs other than educational ones.

Compulsory education ends at age 16 but this does not mean the end of full-time education. All young people have a legal right to education until their 19th birthday.

Well before your son or daughter's 16th birthday, it is important to look at the possibility of continuing education after the age of 16, either at his or her present school or at other local schools or colleges of further education. Youth training schemes may also be able to offer your son or daughter vocational training. People who will be able to help you look into these opportunities are school staff, a specialist careers adviser and organisations such as Skill and RADAR (addresses at the end of this chapter).

WORK OPPORTUNITIES

Ordinary Employment

Some disabled young people are able to enter ordinary employment soon after leaving school, college or Youth Training. There are several schemes to increase employment opportunities for people with disabilities, including financial help towards the cost of getting to and from work, if the young person cannot use public transport and the loaning of special equipment or modified equipment to disabled employees.

The Disability Employment Adviser at your local Job Centre will be able to advise on ordinary employment opportunities for your young person. Remember too that if s/he finds a part-time job of more than 16 hours per week, s/he may be able to get Disability Working Allowances to top up a low wage.

There are some specialist schemes to help disabled young people to get and keep an ordinary job, such as the Pathway Scheme run by MENCAP. Contact MENCAP to see if such a scheme is run in your area.

Sheltered Employment

Sheltered employment is aimed specifically at people with severe disabilities, both physical and learning, who are unlikely to get an ordinary job in open employment. Jobs include work such as packing, gardening, laundry or furniture-making.

Sheltered employment is provided in workshops and factories by Remploy Ltd., (address at the end of this chapter) local authorities and voluntary agencies.

The Sheltered Employment Scheme enables severely disabled people to work in open, ordinary employment alongside other non-disabled people, with support from a sponsoring body.

For more details on all of these opportunities, ask the specialist careers officer at your local Careers Service or the Disability Employment Adviser at your local Job Centre.

Day Centres

Adult training centres (ATCs), or social education centres, are run by social services departments for people with learning disabilities. They offer job training and work experience; basic education; arts and craft work; independent living skills, such as using public transport, shopping, home management; and leisure and recreational activities.

Day centres also exist for young people with physical disabilities. They may offer similar activities and industrial work and job training.

Transport is normally provided for attendance at day centres and attendance can often be combined with a course at a local college.

To arrange a place at a day centre, you should discuss the possibility with your son or daughter's school and with the specialist careers officer. You could also ask a social worker at your local social services department office.

ACCOMMODATION

Independent Living

Specially adapted homes for people with physical disabilities can be provided by local authority housing departments and housing associations. If someone needs a considerable amount of care to live independently because they have physical and/or learning disabilities, it may be possible to obtain live in care from Community Service Volunteers through their Independent Living Schemes. There are also several types of care attendant schemes, where a helper visits regularly during the day and evening. Schemes may be run by the Crossroads Care Attendant Schemes or the Leonard Cheshire Foundation Family Support Service. There are also some local authority care schemes. Ask your social service department for more details. You will need to see someone from the team working with adults with disabilities.

Residential Provision

Living in a residential home with other young people with disabilities may be a more suitable option for those people who need more care, help and supervision.

Residential homes are run by social services departments, housing associations and other voluntary agencies, such as MENCAP. Contact your social services office and voluntary agency to see what is available in your area.

You can also contact CARESEARCH (for people with learning disabilities) or CAREMATCH (for people with physical disabilities) to find suitable residential care. They will take the details of the young person and their needs and then match them up to suitable homes, for which a small charge is made.

There are also a number of voluntary organisations throughout the country which provide long-term accommodation.

Bear in mind, however, that these homes and those offered by CARESEARCH or CAREMATCH will be expensive. Under the new community care legislation that came into effect in April 1993, those wanting to go into residential accommodation have to apply to their social services department for help with fees (previously it was the Department of Social Security). People now have to pass a 'needs test' as well as a 'means test'. It is probably as well to apply to the social services department for an assessment, therefore, before finding out what may be available in case you find that the options are just not affordable.

Another option is a very helpful scheme run by MENCAP: called the Homes Foundation. This provides small family sized homes in ordinary houses which have been left by parents for their disabled sons and daughters. MENCAP also run a Visitors Service which provides a visitor who will keep in touch with a disabled person after his or her parents die. Further details of both schemes are available from MENCAP.

SEXUALITY AND RELATIONSHIPS

A disabled young person's developing sexuality is often an area of great concern to parents. Many parents find it hard to believe that their son or daughter - because they have a learning disability - has sexual needs and

93

sometimes feel that the idea of sex has been put into their minds by staff at school or day centres.

It is important to remember, however, that once your disabled son or daughter has reached his or her teens, physical changes will occur as with any other young adult, and with it the need for sexual fulfilment and close intimate relationships. Schools and day centres will hold lessons on sex education and relationships. It is important that your son or daughter is able to attend and make use of these sessions: being ignorant of sex will not make the need go away so it is best that s/he learns as much as possible about sexuality, relationships and the importance of contraception and so on.

A very good organisation which you may want to contact is SPOD (Association to Aid the Sexual and Personal Relationships of People with a Disability). It has leaflets on all aspects of personal relationships and sex education. SPOD also offers and counselling and runs courses on the sexual aspects of disability.

Another organisation which has information on sex and disability is the Family Planning Association. They also run courses on sex education and personal relationships which are geared to the needs of disabled people. Find out what is on in your area by contacting the Family Planning Association (address at the end of this chapter).

REGISTERING AS A DISABLED PERSON

There are two types of register for disabled people: the local authority register and the disabled person's register.

The Local Authority Register

Every local authority has to keep a register of disabled adults under the Chonically Sick and Disabled Persons Act. Registration is voluntary but there is nothing to lose by registering. In fact, registration will help you get access to some services, such as a travel permit and a telephone. Children can also register to obtain this type of help. Ask your local social services office for details about registering.

Under the Children Act 1989, local authorities also have to set up registers of disabled children. This is to aid planning for future services, and for this reason it is is important that you register your child, although it is voluntary and will not mean that you get a better access to services.

The Disabled Person Register

This is a register kept by the Disability Employment Adviser at the Job Centre of disabled people who are able to work and wish to do so. Young people aged between 16 and 18 can join the register at the Careers Office. Registration is voluntary but may be beneficial for several reasons: a) every employer with 20 or more workers has a duty to employ a proportion of registered disabled people; b) sheltered employment is generally reserved for registered disabled people; c) registered disabled people can be helped to take up an ordinary job, including help with fares to and from work, special equipment, adaptations of premises or equipment, and a personal reader for people with visual impairment; d) vacancies for car park attendants and passenger lift attendants are reserved for registered disabled people.

PARENTS AND LETTING GO

When any young person reaches adolescence, a parent must start the emotional process of letting go of their child. Their son or daughter is no longer completely dependent on them, a parent's role needs to change and their relationship with their son or daughter needs to be reassessed and re-evaluated. For some parents, this time is met with a sense of relief; for others, it represents a strong sense of loss.

These issues present themselves when a disabled young person reaches his or her teenage years, but perhaps to a greater extent. Parents have to grapple with their young person's physical changes, their developing sexuality and independence, whilst at the same time still needing to take much of the initiative in regard to sorting out his or her future education, work and living options.

Most parents, understandably, feel anxious about their disabled son or daughter moving away from home. Some parents never consider this to be an option and continue caring for their son or daughter until they are too old or unwell to do so. Some parents who feel concerned about this sort of situation arising look at the options earlier on, before any crisis occurs, and then find it extremely hard to let go. If they are older parents, they have probably devoted much of their lives to caring for their disabled son or daughter and cannot see any role or life beyond this.

There are no easy answers to these very real dilemmas. The best parents can do is discuss what they feel and the options available for their son or daughter with a professional, such as a social worker or an adviser at their local voluntary organisation for the disabled. Counselling, information and support are the only things which can help parents in this situation so do not be afraid to be open and honest in requesting help.

KEY POINTS

- At age 16, disabled young people can claim benefits in their own right, regardless of their parents' income or savings. Benefits that can be claimed are Severe Disablement Allowance, Income Support and Disability Living Allowance/Disabled Persons Tax Credit.

- All young people have a right to education up to the age of 19. Talk to your son or daughter's school and the specialist careers adviser about the options, which may include staying on at school, attending a college or day centre or Youth Training.

- Work opportunities include ordinary employment and sheltered employment. Speak to the Disability Employment Adviser at the Job Centre about ordinary jobs and the specialist careers adviser at the Careers Office about sheltered work. Registering as a disabled person at the Job centre may be helpful in gaining ordinary employment.

- Living options include independent living or residential care. Ask your Social Services Department for an assessment.

- Sexuality and relationships are an important part of growing up for all young people, including those who are disabled. Organisations such as SPOD and the Family Planning Association provide information, advice and courses on sex and disability.

- The transition from childhood to adulthood and the possibility of a young person moving away from home can present parents with a complex host of emotions and dilemmas. Talking to someone about these feelings is important as is obtaining information and advice and the options open to your son or daughter. Talk to social services or your local voluntary organisation.

USEFUL ORGANISATIONS

Skill: National Bureau for Students with Disabilities
336 Brixton Road, London, SW9 7AA
0171 274 0565

RADAR (Royal Association for Disability and Rehabilitation)
12 City Forum, 250 City Road, London EC1V 8AF
0171 250 3222

MENCAP (Royal Society for Mentally Handicapped Children and Adults)
123 Golden Lane, London, EC1Y ORT
0171 454 0454

REMPLOY LTD
415 Edgware Road, London NW2 6LR
0181 452 8020

COMMUNITY SERVICE VOLUNTEERS
237 Pentonville Road, London N1 9NJ
0171 278 6601

CROSSROAD CARE ATTENDANT SCHEMES LTD
10 Regent Place, Rugby, Warwicks. CV21 2PN
01788 573653

LEONARD CHESHIRE FOUNDATION
26-29 Maunsel Street, London, SW1P 2QN
0171 828 1822

CAREMATCH
286 Camden Road, London N7 OBJ
0171 609 9966

CARESEARCH
Fairways, the Hudnalls, St Briavels, Lydney, Glos. GL15 6SQ
01594 530220

ACORN VILLAGES
Acorn Village Community, Mistley Hall, Manningtree, Essex, CO1 12NJ
01206 394124

CAMPHILL VILLAGE TRUST
Camphill Village Trust, Delrow House, Hilfield Lane, Aldenham, Watford, WD2 8DJ
01923 856006

L'ARCHE COMMUNITIES
Secretariat, 14 London Road, Beccles, Suffolk, NR34 9NH
01502 715329

SPOD (Association to Aid the Sexual and Personal Relationships of People with a Disability)
286 Camden Road, London N7 OBJ
0171 607 8851

FAMILY PLANNING ASSOCIATION
27-35 Mortimer Street, London W1N 7RJ
0171 636 7866

8

THE LAW AND HOW TO MAKE A COMPLAINT

It is a fact that disabled children and their families have a right to services to improve the quality of their lives. This right is a legal one and is explicit in a number of pieces of legislation, which are outlined in this chapter. Knowing the legislation under which you are entitled to certain services can often help in gaining access to them so do not be afraid to quote the law. It is also important to know how to make a formal and official complaint if necessary. Being in a position of needing to ask for services and help can make you feel powerless: knowing your legal rights and how to complain will give you a little more control over obtaining the help you need. The law is very complex and the descriptions of the relevant legislation given below are very brief and basic. If you need more details or specialist legal advice it is advisable to see someone at your local Citizens Advice Bureau or a Solicitor if you have one.

THE CHILDREN ACT 1989 AND DISABLED CHILDREN

The Children Act 1989, which came into force in October 1991, is the first piece of legislation for children which includes disabled children and at last recognises that children with disabilities are children first.

The Children Act introduces the concept of a child "in need". Children in need include:

(i) children whose health and welfare may suffer significantly without services from the local authority;

(ii) disabled children.

Under the Children Act 1989, a disabled child is a child who is: "blind, deaf or dumb or suffers from mental disorder of any kind or is substantially and permanently handicapped by illness, injury or congenital deformity or such other disability as may be prescribed;"

The local authority which provides services for children includes social services, housing, education and leisure services. Other services which may be offered are provided by the health authority and/or local voluntary organisations.

The local authority must do the following for children in need, including disabled children:

- provide day care for under 5s;

- provide after school and holiday supervised activities;

- set up a register of children with disabilities;

- publish information about services;

- provide services designed to give children with disabilities the opportunity to lead lives which are as normal as possible.

Examples of services depend on what the local authority views as appropriate but may include home helps, family centres, respite care, financial assistance for holidays etc.,

- provide services which take account of a child's race, religion, culture and language

- set up a complaints procedure;

- provide services which protect and promote the welfare of all children, including the duty to investigate all allegations of abuse and/or neglect;

- provide a high standard of care for children who are being looked after by the local authority, in foster or residential homes;

- seek the views of children and parents/carers, when working with families and planning services, and work at all times in partnership with families.

THE EDUCATION ACT 1996 AND SPECIAL EDUCATIONAL NEEDS

The Education Act 1996 specifies the powers and duties of Local Authority Education Departments in providing for the special educational needs (SEN) of children with disabilities.

The main duties of LEAs under the Education Act 1996 is to identify special educational needs of children for whom they are responsible and to make the special educational provision which they need.

Schools and local education authorities are required to have regard to the Code of Practice on the identification and assessment of special educational needs. The Code recommends that schools should identify children's needs and take action to meet those needs as early as possible, working with parents. The Code says that schools should deal with children's needs in stages. These are outlined in chapter four.

THE CHRONICALLY SICK AND DISABLED PERSON'S ACT 1970

Under this piece of legislation, the local authority has a duty to establish numbers of disabled people in their area, to determine their needs and publicise services. It is also the duty of the local authority to arrange any of the following services (where satisfied it is necessary):

- practical assistance in the home;

- help with radio and TV;

- library and recreational facilities;

- help to take up facilities outside the home;

- assistance with travel (permits and orange badge scheme);

- help with holidays, telephones, aids and adaptations.

Finally, the local authority has a duty to provide access for disabled people in certain buildings to which the public have access.

NHS AND COMMUNITY CARE ACT 1990

The Act emphasises a care management approach and assessment based on individual need. It requires a close partnership between professionals and service users in assessing and designing tailor-made packages of care. This piece of legislation emphasises the importance of dividing the purchasing of care from the provision of care, and puts great emphasis on the independent sector to provide social care.

The Act also says that Community Care plans must be published and reviewed by each local authority, in consultation with health authorities, housing and voluntary agencies representing service users and carers.

A needs assessment must be carried out where it appears to the local authority that any person for whom they may provide or arrange community care services, may be in need of such services. Where services of the health or housing authorities may be needed, the local authority should notify them and invite their assistance.

Where a needs assessment has been carried out , the local authority shall then decide whether services should be provided. Care may be provided before a needs assessment, where urgently necessary, with an assessment carried out as soon as possible afterwards.

CARERS (RECOGNITION AND SERVICES) ACT 1995

This Act requires local authorities to assess the needs of carers of disabled people, including disabled children, and people who are chronically sick, including young carers.

HOUSING GRANTS,CONSTRUCTION AND REGENERATION ACT 1996 (ENGLAND AND WALES).

Disabled Facilities Grant

Under Part 1 of the Housing Grants, Construction and Regeneration Act 1996 local housing authorities are able to give Disabled Facilities Grants to disabled people, including disabled children, to help with the cost of adaptations to enable them to live as independently as possible in their own homes.

The main underlying principle is that disabled people should be able to enjoy comparable facilities in their homes to those enjoyed by able-bodied people. The grant is therefore designed to address the adaptation needs to which a person's ability gives rise by providing:

- mandatory grant for adaptation works of an essential nature up to £20,000 in England and £24,000 in Wales

- discretionary grant for a wide range of works which go beyond basic housing requirements

The purposes for which the Mandatory Disabled Facilities Grant can be given are:

- facilitating access to and from the dwelling

- facilitating access to living rooms, bedrooms and bathroom in the dwelling and facilitating use of facilities in bathroom

- facilitating preparation and cooking of food by a disabled person

- improving the heating system in the dwelling and facilitating use by a disabled person of control over sources of power, heat or light

- making the dwelling safe for the disabled occupant and others residing with him or her

A discretionary Disabled Facilities Grant can be given to make a dwelling suitable for the accommodation, welfare or employment of a disabled person or to "top up" the grant for a mandatory adaptation costing more than £20,000 in England or £24,000 in Wales.

A local authority is only able to approve a Disabled Facilities Grant where it is satisfied that the works are suitable to meet the disabled persons needs. The amount of grant awarded is subject to a means test. For disabled children or young people up to their 18t^h birthday the "test of resources" is applied to the joint income of both parents if they live together, or to the child's main carer. 18 year olds and young people of 16 or 17 claiming benefits in their own right will be assessed on their own income. Housing authorities must ensure the works for which the grant are sought are "necessary and appropriate" to meet the needs of a disabled person/child. The local authority must also decide if it is "reasonable and practicable" to carry them out in a particular dwelling. If it is impracticable other options (such as re-housing) may need to be explored.

HOW TO MAKE A COMPLAINT

Health

If you have a problem with your G.P., it is best to discuss this with the surgery first. If you want to take the matter further, you should contact the Family Health Services Authority (FHSA), Health Board in Scotland or

Health and Social Services Board in Northern Ireland. The address will be in your local telephone directory. You could also contact your local Community Health Council (CHC), Local Health Council in Scotland or District Committee for Health and Social Services in Northern Ireland.

If you have a complaint about treatment you or your child has received in hospital, you should try and deal with it in stages: first, it is best to discuss the complaint informally with a member of staff; second, if your complaint cannot be dealt with informally you could take it to a complaints officer in the hospital, if they have one; third, if there is not a complaints officer or you are still not satisfied, you could write to the Chief Executive of the local Health Trust. You should also ask your local Community Health Council advice on doing this. Another avenue is the NHS Ombudsman, who investigates complaints to do with maladministration. Remember also that there is now a Health Service Patients' charter, which you can use when making a complaint.

Education

When dealing with your Local Education Authority (LEA), if at any stage you are unhappy with a decision, you should talk to your child's school or to the Named Officer who has dealt with your child's case. However, if you cannot come to an agreement with the LEA and/or you wish to make a complaint, you have a right to take the matter to the Special Educational Needs Tribunal.

You can appeal to the Special Educational Needs Tribunal if:

the LEA refuse to make a statutory assessment of your child, after you have asked them to;

the LEA refuse to make a statement for your child after an assessment;

you disagree with parts 2,3 or 4 of your child's statement;

your child already has a statement and the LEA refuse to assess your child again or change the name of the school in that statement;

the LEA decide to stop maintaining your child's statement.

More information about the Special Educational Needs Tribunal can be obtained from your local LEA, in the form of a booklet.

Social Services

Since April 1991 all Social Services Departments have had to set up a formal complaints procedure. Your complaint will be investigated by an officer of the council and an independent person, who will both talk to you and any other relevant parties about your situation. The result of the investigation should be given to you in writing, after which you may take the matter further to the Independent Review Panel if you are still not satisfied. Ask your local Social Services Department for details on how to use the procedure.

Housing

If you want to make a complaint about a housing matter which is related to a disability, such as a delay in doing adaptations to your home, for example, RADAR may be able to help you make a complaint. You could also contact the Local Government Ombudsman if there has been any maladministration.

Further help with making a complaint

When making a complaint about health, education, social services, housing or any other issue, you could try and contact your local councillor or M.P. You will be able to find our how to do this by contacting your local council or by asking at your local Citizens Advice Bureau, who may also be able to help with your complaint.

Now read the key points from chapter 8.

KEY POINTS

- Knowing your legal rights and how to make a complaint can help give you more control over the services you and your disabled child receive.

- You and your child have a right to services under the Children Act 1989, the Education Act 1996, the Chronically Sick and Disabled Persons Act 1970, the NHS and Community Care Act 1990.the Carers Act 1995 and the Housing Grants and Reconstruction Act (1996).

- Making a complaint is sometimes necessary and can often help improve services for other disabled children and their families. Most council departments and the health service have their own procedures but there are outside bodies you can use, such as the Community Health Council, the Special Educational Needs Tribunal and your local councillor or M.P. The Citizens Advice Bureau may also be able to advise you.

USEFUL ORGANISATIONS

Children's Legal Centre
University of Essex
Wivenhoe Park
Colchester
Essex CO4 3SQ
01206 873820 (advice line 2-5 pm)

Disability Law Centre
16 Princeton Street
London WC1R 4BB
0171 831 8031

Advisory Centre for Education and
the Education Law Association
1b Aberdeen Studios
22 Highbury Grove
London N5 2EA
0171 354 8318

RADAR (Royal Association for Disability and Rehabilitation)
12 City Forum
250 City Road
London EC1V 8AF
0171 250 3222

Local Authority Ombudsmen
Commission for Local Administration in England
21 Queen Anne's Gate
London SW1H 9BU
0171 915 3210

The Oaks
Westwood Way
Westwood Business Park
Coventry CV4 8JB
01203 69599

Beverley House
17 Shipton Road
York YO3 6FZ
01904 630151

Commission for Local Administration in Wales
Derwen House
Court Road
Bridgend
Wales CF31 1BN
01656 661325

Commissioner for Local Administration in Scotland
23 Walker Street
Edinburgh EH3 7HX
0131 225 5300

Commissioner for Complaints
Progressive House
33 Wellington Place
Belfast BT1 6HN
01232 233821

Health Service Ombudsman

England: Church House
Great Smith Street
London SW1P 3BW
0171 276 3000

Scotland: 11 Melville Crescent
Edinburgh EH3 7LU
0131 225 7465

Wales: Pearl Assurance House
Greyfriars Road
Cardiff CF1 3AG
01222 394621

Northern Ireland: Office of N.I. Commissioner for Complaints
33 Wellington Place
Belfast BT2 6HN
01232 233821

Useful Reading

CHAPTER ONE - REACTIONS AND EMOTIONS - AND GENERAL

Taking Care   Alison Cowen, Joseph Rowntree Foundation 1994

Special Needs Special Children Mary McCormack, Thorsons 1992

Children with Special Needs Richard Woolfson, Faber and Faber 1991

CHAPTER TWO - WHO CAN HELP? WHO DOES WHAT?

Who's Who in the Health and Allied Services Contact a Family, Fact Sheet.

Speech and Language Therapy for Children with a Learning Disability MENCAP, Fact Sheet.

You and Your Child   MENCAP, Fact Sheet.

CHAPTER THREE - FINANCES

Disability Benefits Contact a Family, Fact Sheet

Disability Rights Handbook Disability Alliance

Benefits Checklist Family Fund, Fact Sheet.

What Can You Claim? MENCAP, Fact Sheet

Leaving Money by Will to People with Learning Disabilities MENCAP.

CHAPTER FOUR - EDUCATION

Special Education Handbook ACE

A Parents Guide to Statements of Special Educational Needs   Contact a Family Fact Sheet

Special Educational Needs A Guide for Parents Department for Education.

Special Educational Needs: A Guide for Parents MENCAP

CHAPTER FIVE - BREAKS AND HOLIDAYS

Holidays   Contact a Family, Fact Sheet.

Holidays   Family Fund, Fact Sheet.

Holidays and Travel Abroad RADAR

Holidays in the British Isles RADAR

Sport and Outdoor Activity Holidays RADAR

Holiday Insurance   RADAR

Holiday Finance RADAR

A Guide to Financial Help Towards the Cost of a Holiday Holiday Care Service.

Respite Care Resource Pack MENCAP.

117

CHAPTER SIX - TRANSPORT AND EQUIPMENT

Door to Door Guide to Transport for Disabled People
Department of Transport

Transport Family Fund, Fact Sheet.

Equipment for Daily Living   Family Fund, Fact Sheet.

Adaptations to Housing Family Fund, Fact Sheet.

CHAPTER SEVEN - TOWARDS ADULTHOOD

After Age 16 What Next? Services and Benefits for Young Disabled
People

Family Fund.

Growing Up and Sexuality Contact a Family.

Sexuality and Young People with Learning Difficulties

Contact a Family.

Into Work: A Guide for Disabled People   RADAR

MENCAP Colleges   MENCAP, Fact Sheet.

MENCAP Visitors Scheme   MENCAP, Fact Sheet.

Letting Go   Ann Richardson and Jane Ritchie,
Open University Press 1989

118

Making the Break   Ann Richardson and Jane Ritchie,
King's Fund   1986

After I've Gone - What will Happen to my Handicapped Child? Gerald
Sanctuary , Human Horizon   1991

**CHAPTER EIGHT - THE LAW AND HOW TO MAKE A
COMPLAINT**

Disabled Children and Legislation   Barnardos.

Making Sense of the Children Act 1989   Nick Allen   Longman   1990

Acts of Parliament Relevant to People with a Learning
Disability MENCAP, Fact Sheet.

Useful Organisations

Each chapter has a list of useful organisations relevant to that particular topic or topics. This list comprises the main national organisations you may find useful, some of which have already been mentioned in other chapters.

Action for Sick Children (NAWCH)
Argyle House, 29-31 Euston Road, London NW1 2SD
0171 833 2041

Association for All Speech Impaired Children (AFASIC)
347 Central Market, Smithfield, London EC1A 9HN
0171 236 3632/6487

Association for Spina Bifida and Hydrocephalus (ASBAH)
42 Park Road, Peterborough, PE1 2UQ
01733 555988

British Association of Cancer United Patients (BACUP)
121-123 Charterhouse Street, London EC1M 6AA
0171 608 1785

British Dyslexia Association
98 London Road, Reading, RG1 5AU
01734 668271

British Epilepsy Association
Anstey House, 40 Hanover Square, Leeds LS3 1BE
01532 439393

Brittle Bone Society
Ward 8, Strathmartine Hospital, Strathmartine, Dundee DD3 OPG
01382 817771

Carers' National Association
20 Glasshouse Yard, London EC1A 4JN
0171 490 8818 Carers' Line: 0171 490 8898

The Council for Disabled Children
8 Wakley Street, London EC1V 7QE
0171 843 6000

Contact a Family
170 Tottenham Court Road, London W1P 0HA
0171 383 3555

Cystic Fibrosis Research Trust
Alexandra House, 5 Blyth Road, Bromley, Kent BR1 3RS
0181 464 7211
Department for Education Publications Centre
P.O. Box 6927
London E3 3NZ
0171 510 0150

Department of Transport
Disability Unit
Room S 10/21
2 Marsham Street
London SW1V 3EB
0171 276 3000

Disability Alliance
Universal House, Wentworth Street, London E1 &SA
0171 247 8776

Down's Syndrome Association
153 Mitcham Road, London SW17 9PG
0181 682 4001

Family Fund
P.O. Box 50, York, YO1 1UY
01904 621115

Freidreich's Ataxia Group
The Common, Cranleigh, Surrey, GU8 8SB
01483 272741

Hyperactive Children's Support Group
71 Whyke Lane, Chichester, Sussex
01903 725183

MENCAP (Royal Society for Mentally Handicapped Children and Adults)
123 Golden Lane, London EC1Y ORT
0171 253 9433

Muscular Dystrophy Group
Prescott House, Prescott Place, London SW4 2BS
0171 720 8055

National Autistic Society
276 Willesden Lane, London, NW2 5RB
0181 451 1114

SENSE (National Deaf-Blind and Rubella Association)
Laurel Leaf House, Clifton Terrace, London N4 3SR
0171 272 7774

National Deaf Children's Society
15 Dufferin Street, London, EC1Y 8PD
0171 250 0123

National Eczema Society
Tavistock House East, Tavistock Square, London WC1H 9SR
0171 388 4097

National Federation of Gateway Clubs
117 Golden Lane, London EC1Y ORT
0171 253 9433

Royal National Institute for the Blind (RNIB)
224 Great Portland Street, London W1N 6AA
0171 388 1266

Royal National Institute for Deaf People (RNID)
105 Gower Street, London WC1E 6AH
0171 387 8033

Sickle Cell Society
Palmerston Court, Palmerston Way, London SW8 4DA
0171 720 2081

SCOPE
12 Park Crescent, London, W1N 4EQ
0171 636 5020

Helpline: 0800 626216 Monday to Friday 11am-9pm, Saturday and Sunday 2-6pm

Tuberous Sclerosis Association
Martell Mount, Holywell Road, Malvern, Wells, Worcestershire, WR14 4LF
016845 631505

INDEX

A

B

D

E

I

J

K

L

M

N

O

P

Pre-school Playgroups Association 63
Psychologist 33

- see educational and clinical psychologist

Q

R

RADAR 70 75 77 85 90 99 112
Reactions
- see emotions
Registers
- children with disabilities 32
- Disabled Person Register (Job Centre) 94
Relate 16 23
Remploy Ltd 99
Respite care 32 65 67
Road tax exemption 44 79
Royal National Institute for the Blind 123
Royal National Institute for Deaf People 123

S

SCOPE 123
Segregation
-    in education 59
-    SENSE (National Deaf-Blind & Rubella Assoc.) 123
Severe Disablement Allowance 87
Sexuality 93
Shared Care UK 77
Short-term breaks 32 65 68

W

welfare benefits
- Income Support 37 87 88
- premiums 38
- help with NHS treatment 38
- Disability Living Allowance 39 87
- Disability Working Allowance 89
- Family Credit 42
- Social Fund 43
- road tax exemption 44
- housing benefit 44 89
- council tax benefit 44
- help with transport 79
- Severe Disablement Allowance 87
Wheelchairs 82
Wills
- leaving money to a learning disabled person 46